The History of Montréal

BY THE SAME AUTHOR

Quebec: A History 1867-1929. Toronto: 1983 (with R. Durocher and J.-C. Robert).

The Promoters' City: Building the Industrial Town of Maisonneuve, 1883-1918. Toronto: 1985.

Nouvelle histoire du Québec et du Canada. Montreal, CEC, 1985 (with L. Charpentier, C. Laville and R. Durocher).

Quebec Since 1930. Toronto: 1991 (with R. Durocher, J.-C. Robert and F. Ricard).

Histoire de Montréal depuis la Confédération. Montreal: 1992, 2000.

Clés pour l'histoire de Montréal. Bibliographie. Montreal: 1992 (with J. Burgess, L. Dechêne and J.-C. Robert).

Histoire du Canada. Paris: 1994-2010.

Barcelona-Montréal. Desarollo urbano comparado / Développement urbain comparé. Barcelona: 1998 (with Horacio Capel, eds.).

Vers la construction d'une citoyenneté canadienne. Paris: 2006 (with J.-M. Lacroix, eds.).

Vivre en ville. Bruxelles et Montréal (xixe-xxe siècles). Brussels: 2006 (with S. Jaumain. eds.).

France-Canada-Québec. 400 ans de relations d'exception. Montreal: 2008 (with S. Joyal, eds.).

Sainte-Catherine Street: At the Heart of Montreal Life. Montreal: 2010.

Place Ville Marie: Montreal's Shining Landmark. Montreal: 2012 (with F. Vanlaethem, S. Marchand, and J.-A. Chartrand).

Paul-André Linteau

The History
of Montréal

The Story of a Great North American City

Translated by Peter McCambridge

Baraka
Books
Montréal

Originally published as *Brève histoire de Montréal*
© 2007 by Les éditions du Boréal
Publié avec l'autorisation de Les éditions du Boréal, Montréal, Québec

Translation Copyright © Baraka Books 2013

Library and Archives Canada Cataloguing in Publication

Linteau, Paul-André, 1946-

The history of Montréal: the story of a great North American city / Paul-André Linteau; translated by Peter McCambridge.

Translation of: Brève histoire de Montréal.
Includes bibliographical references and index.
Issued also in electronic formats.
ISBN 978-1-926824-77-2 (pbk); 978-1-926824-81-9 (epub); 978-1-926824-80-2 (pdf); 978-1-926824-82-6 (mobi/kindle)

1. Montréal (Québec)–History. I. Title.

FC2947.4.L55313 2013   971.4'28   C2013-900715-6

ISBN 978-1-926824-77-2 pbk; 978-1-926824-81-9 epub; 978-1-926824-81-9 pdf; 978-1-926824-81-9 mobi/kindle

Cover by Folio infographie
Book design by Folio Infographie
Translated by Peter McCambridge

Legal Deposit, 2nd quarter 2013

Bibliothèque et Archives nationales du Québec
Library and Archives Canada

Published by Baraka Books of Montreal.
6977, rue Lacroix
Montréal, Québec H4E 2V4
Telephone: 514 808-8504
info@barakabooks.com
www.barakabooks.com

Printed and bound in Quebec

Baraka Books acknowledges the generous support of its publishing program from the Société de développement des entreprises culturelles du Québec (SODEC) and the Canada Council for the Arts.

We acknowledge the financial support of the Government of Canada, through the National Translation Program for Book Publishing for our translation activities and through the Canada Book Fund (CBF) for our publishing activities.

Trade Distribution & Returns
Canada and the United States
Independent Publishers Group
1-800-888-4741 (IPG1);
orders@ipgbook.com

Contents

COVER PHOTOS

Publisher's Foreword

Montreal has always fascinated people throughout the world. Yet, nearly forty-five years have gone by since the last accessible short history of Montreal appeared in English, *Montreal: A Brief History* by Cooper published in 1969. So much has changed since then, not the least of which is the way we study, read and understand history. Professor Paul-André Linteau ensured that French-speaking readers could read the story of Montreal when he wrote the original book, *Brève histoire de Montréal*, first published in 1992 to mark the city's 350th anniversary and then updated in 2007. Surprisingly, however, the book did not appear in English until now. In itself, that absence fully justifies publishing this book.

Yet there are so many other reasons to bring out a good short history of Montreal. People have written about this city extensively, often enthusiastically, sometimes romantically, occasionally disparagingly, but never indifferently. Fascination for the city and its inhabitants dates back many centuries.

In 1535, Jacques Cartier glowingly described Montreal's predecessor, the Iroquoian village of Hochelaga and the country surrounding it, now the island of Montreal, as "the finest and most excellent one could find anywhere… fine land with large fields covered with corn of the country." He also lavished praise on the people who welcomed him and on how their village was organized. During his travels in the seventeenth century, Samuel de Champlain also vaunted the site of the future city.

The Swedish botanist Pehr Kalm, in his 1749 travelogue originally published in Latin, provides detailed descriptions of the town's fortifications, its churches and wide streets, its lively weekly market, but also its people, and particularly the women. Contrasting the ladies in Montreal with those in Quebec and in France, he wrote: "Even the French reproach the ladies in Montreal for their immodesty, like that of Indian women, and their lack of instruction."

One hundred years later, Henry David Thoreau brilliantly captured the feeling of Montreal in his book *A Yankee in Canada* published after he visited Canada in 1850.

This city makes the more favourable impression from being approached by water, and also being built of stone, a gray limestone found on the island... it made on me the impression of a seaport. (...) Montreal makes the impression of a larger city than you had expected to find, though you may have heard that it contains nearly sixty thousand inhabitants. In the newer parts it appeared to be growing fast like a small New York, and to be considerably Americanized. The names of the squares reminded you of Paris,—the Champ de mars, the Place d'Armes, and others,—and you felt as if a French revolution might break out any moment. Glimpses of Mount Royal rising behind the town, and the names of some streets in that direction, make one think of Edinburgh.

Jackie Robinson came to Montreal one hundred years after Thoreau, not as a Yankee but as an African-American baseball player about to revolutionize professional sports. Jackie Robinson and his family loved Montreal and talked about it regularly. To the CBC he declared, "Fortunately I broke in (to professional baseball) in a city like Montreal. We have a tremendously warm spot for that city because they treated us so well… The fact that I played in Montreal had a great deal to do with the success I had."

Quotes about Montreal over the centuries are so numerous that it would take another book to do them justice. And yet we would still not know what makes the city so interesting.

Who better therefore than Paul-André Linteau to take on that challenge? Who better than he to explain the forces and circumstances that have made Montreal what it is, one of those unique cities that has been—and will likely continue to be—at the crossroads of history? Professor Linteau has devoted much of his life to studying the history of Montreal, writing about it in popular and academic publications, teaching it to university students, and giving talks about it in Canada and abroad. This book is a result of those many years of teaching and research, but is also based on the works of hundreds of authors who have explored the diverse aspects of Montreal's past. A special thanks for their help is also extended to Mario Robert, who heads the Archives at the City of Montreal, and Jean-Claude Robert, Emeritus Professor at the Université du Québec à Montréal.

As Montreal prepares to celebrate in 2017 the 375th anniversary of its founding, Baraka Books is proud to join forces with Paul-André Linteau to publish *The History of Montréal, The Story of a Great North American City*.

Robin Philpot

List of Illustrations and Maps

CHAPTER 1

Hochelaga

Montreal was born in 1642, but the area's history obviously dates back much further. And yet knowledge of this part of the city's past remains, even today, far from complete. We know that the island was frequented—and even inhabited—by Iroquoian people before the French arrived, but experts do not agree on what happened to these first populations.[1]

An enviable location

To understand the reasons that led to groups settling, temporarily or permanently, on the island of Montreal, first we need to take a closer look at the island. Thousands of years ago, only the summit of Mount Royal peeked out above the waters of the Champlain Sea. As the waters retreated, the mountain acted as an anchor for the land that formed the island of Montreal, and remains a focal point of the cityscape today.

---

1. In the past, in Montreal, many French names were translated into English. Saint-Laurent suburb was also known as St. Lawrence suburb, rue Saint-Jacques as St. James Street and so on. This practice officially disappeared some decades ago. Accordingly, in line with current usage, we have chosen to use the French spelling of place names throughout the book. Also since readers who are in Montreal will see "rue Sainte-Catherine" and not "Sainte-Catherine Street," words like "street" and "boulevard" are written in lower case.

The St. Lawrence River played an even greater role in shaping Montreal's history. All around the world, mighty rivers have cradled civilizations, favouring the emergence of great cities, especially for centuries when water was the main means of transporting people and goods over long distances. The St. Lawrence was no exception. But why did Montreal and not Sorel or Trois-Rivières become the biggest city along the river? As we will see later, this can partly be explained by the city's history as a whole, as well as the constraints of geography.

Coming from the Atlantic, travellers along the St. Lawrence hit a major obstacle at Montreal: the Lachine rapids. Goods had to be unloaded and portaged all the way to Lachine, with things being no better for those heading the other way. This obligation to unload and reload boats would make Montreal's fortune over the years.

Prehistoric Montreal was likely a temporary camp for groups passing through the St. Lawrence Valley. With game, fish, and berries in abundance, it even offered ready access to food. Yet there is scant archaeological evidence of human activity on the prehistoric island of Montreal. We know that occupation of the St. Lawrence Valley began some 6,000 years ago, but artifacts uncovered beneath the city seem to date back no further than a handful of centuries before the Europeans arrived. It is plausible that the island was frequented long before, but this has never been proven. Nor do we know exactly when Aboriginal peoples permanently settled on the island of Montreal. What we do know is that in 1535, when French explorer Jacques Cartier travelled across the island, he found a sedentary population living in a large village: Hochelaga.

The Iroquoians

These people were part of a group known as the St. Lawrence Iroquoians. The St. Lawrence Iroquoians belonged to the broad linguistic family of the Iroquoians, along with other nations like the Hurons and the Iroquois, but were a distinct people. Little is known about their origins. The St. Lawrence Iroquoians are thought to have formed a specific cultural group around 1300, and are believed to have emerged from groups previously established in the area. Specialists have observed differences within this people, particularly between the groups that settled around Quebec and Montreal.

The St. Lawrence Iroquoians, like the Hurons and the Iroquois, were sedentary and lived mainly from agriculture. They mostly grew corn, but also beans, squash, and tobacco. They fished and hunted to complete their diet, and traded with Algonquin hunter-gatherers, exchanging corn for fur pelts and meat.

Women had an important role to play in their society and were the heads of families and clans. They farmed the land and made pottery decorated with original motifs that illustrated the distinct culture of the St. Lawrence Iroquoians.

The Iroquoians lived in villages surrounded by wooden stockades, with some of the biggest villages boasting more than a thousand inhabitants. They built huge oblong-shaped houses, shared by families from the same clan. The houses were made from wood lattice covered with bark. Farmed fields surrounded their villages. After 10 to 20 years, when the fields had grown less fertile, the Iroquoians would move their villages, usually to somewhere nearby.

The village of Hochelaga described by Cartier broadly resembled this description. It was surrounded by a high stockade to which walkways were attached, enabling the village's defenders to throw projectiles at attackers. Access to the village was through a single gate. Inside, Cartier saw some 50 houses, 50 paces long and 12 to 15 paces wide. Each was divided into separate living areas for each family and had a central fireplace for cooking food. Cartier estimated the village to be home to one thousand souls, but judging by the number and dimensions of the houses, ethnologist Bruce Trigger believes 1,500 to be a likelier estimate. Here is how Cartier described Hochelaga:

> And in the middle of these fields is situated and stands the village of Hochelaga, near and adjacent to a mountain, the slopes of which are fertile and are cultivated, and from the top of which one can see for a long distance. We named this mountain "Mount Royal." The village is circular and is completely enclosed by a wooden palisade in three tiers like a pyramid. The top one is built crosswise, the middle one perpendicular and the lowest one of strips of wood placed lengthwise. The whole is well joined and lashed after their manner, and is some two lances in height. There is only one gate and entrance to this village, and that can be barred up. Over this gate and in many places about the enclosure are species of galleries with ladders for mounting to them, which galleries are provided with rocks and stones for the defence and protection of the place. There are some fifty houses in this village, (...) built completely of wood and covered in and bordered up with large pieces of the bark and rind of trees, as broad as a table, which are well and cunningly lashed after their manner. (From H.P. Biggar, *The Voyages of Jacques Cartier: published from the originals with translations, notes, and appendices*, Ottawa, 1924.)

So where was Hochelaga? It remains a mystery to this day. According to Cartier, it was close to the mountain. In the nineteenth century, remains of an Iroquoian village were discovered—the Dawson site—south of Sherbrooke, opposite McGill University. But it was much smaller than the site described by the French explorer and probably another village, perhaps a satellite of Hochelaga.

Everything hangs, obviously, on how we interpret Cartier's words. If, as most specialists believe, Cartier approached the island from the St. Lawrence side, then Hochelaga was probably somewhere between today's Sherbrooke street and the mountain. If, as Quebec architect and history buff Aristide Beaugrand-Champagne maintained, he came along Rivière des Prairies (sometimes called the Back river in English), then the village would be on the other side of the mountain. Which means that, unless new archaeological discoveries advance the debate, the question surrounding the village's location will remain unanswered. But one thing is for sure: there was no direct correlation between the location of Hochelaga and the town of Montreal to come, since the latter would be built on the shores of the St. Lawrence.

Cartier returned to Montreal in 1541. His notes from the voyage mention two Iroquoian villages along the St. Lawrence. They were probably temporary fishing camps, one close to Sainte-Marie Current (near what is now the Jacques-Cartier Bridge), the other close to the Lachine rapids. This time there was no mention of Hochelaga, but the town of Tutonaguy, which Cartier did not visit. Might it have been another name for Hochelaga (or perhaps even the village's real name, with Hochelaga the name for the area as a whole?) or a village that replaced Hochelaga? The question has never been answered to anyone's complete satisfaction.

What should we take away from all of this? In the sixteenth century, and perhaps before, the island of Montreal was home to at least one major permanent settlement inhabited by the St. Lawrence Iroquoians. By 1603, when Champlain explored the St. Lawrence, the Iroquoians no longer lived in Montreal or anywhere else in the St. Lawrence Valley. Many have tried to explain their disappearance. A series of poor harvests caused by bad weather could have forced them to move. Illnesses introduced by the French, against which they were defenceless, might have thinned their ranks. Most of all it is highly probable that they were attacked by their traditional enemies the Hurons, the Algonquins, or the Iroquois. Keen to join the burgeoning fur trade with the French at the end of the sixteenth century, these rivals might have cast aside the St. Lawrence Iroquoians who controlled the river, the main means of travel. A combination of these factors might have led to the dispersal of the St. Lawrence Iroquoians. And it is possible that some of the survivors were integrated into other Aboriginal groups. The end result was that at the start of the seventeenth century, Montreal no longer had a permanent settlement, even though the island remained a hub that hunting groups, war parties, and trading expeditions would pass through.

A visit from the French

The sudden arrival of the French clearly upset the environmental, economic, and political balance of the St. Lawrence Valley. And yet it had taken over a century for them to settle permanently on the island of Montreal. What had they been up to before 1642?

Jacques Cartier was the first Frenchman and the first European to set foot on the island's shores. He arrived in October 1535 and spent no more than a day in Montreal. He had no interpreter with him, meaning that he was unable to use the information the inhabitants shared with him. One of Cartier's biggest contributions to history was the account he wrote of his visit to the village of Hochelaga. He also wrote an initial description of the area, even though he did not realize it was an island. And he made a lasting contribution to the island's toponymy, christening the mountain "Mont Royal," a name that would be extended to the whole of the island since Montreal is simply another way of writing Mont Royal, *réal* being synonymous with *royal*. He also made the name Hochelaga more widely known, a familiar sight in place names around the city to this day.

During his second and final trip to the island in September 1541 (which was just as brief as the first), Cartier did not add much to his knowledge of Montreal, although this time he went right up to the foot of the Lachine rapids. In 1543, Roberval also travelled as far as Montreal, but nothing is known of his voyage, other than the fact that he too probably went to the Lachine rapids. Around 1585, a nephew of Cartier's, Jacques Noël, retraced his uncle's steps and scaled Mount Royal, without unearthing any new information.

It was not until Samuel de Champlain that the French were again in contact with Montreal. In 1603, it was Champlain's turn to travel up the St. Lawrence to the Lachine rapids. His local guides provided him with detailed information on the land upstream from Montreal, particularly the course of the St. Lawrence as far as Lake Huron and the role the Ottawa River played in transporting goods inland. This gave him a much better idea than his predecessors of Montreal's enviable position at the confluence of both commercial axes.

It took until 1611, three years after he founded Quebec, for Champlain to grow more interested in the island's potential. He spent several weeks there trading furs and used the occasion to explore the surrounding area. He could see the benefits of setting up a trading post on the island and chose the very same site—today known as Pointe-à-Callière—chosen by Maisonneuve and his group 31 years later. Champlain cleared a space, which he named Place Royale, then had a wall built and prepared and seeded two gardens. On a map that he published in 1613, he referred to the island by the name of Montreal for the very first time.

Over the next few years, Montreal became a meeting place for Aboriginals and French traders. The Aboriginals arrived in groups over the summer, canoes laden with furs from the *Pays d'en haut* (the *upper country* encompassing the entire Great Lakes), which they exchanged for European products. Champlain's goal of setting up a permanent trading post there never came to fruition, however. There were simply not enough Frenchmen to maintain two separate settlements, one at Quebec, the other at Montreal. They had to make do with a presence on the island for only part of the year.

Another factor weighing against a permanent settlement on the island was the growing threat from the Iroquois. Champlain had allied with the Algonquins and Hurons and joined in a number of their war parties against the Iroquois. But the Iroquois, particularly the Mohawks, known as *Agniers* in French, were remarkable warriors, capable not only of keeping their enemies at bay, but of launching attacks of their own. They also became involved in the fur trade, not with the French, but with the Dutch merchants of Nieuw-Nederland (later the colony of New York). Their objective was clear: to control the flow of furs along the St. Lawrence by eliminating the competition.

The handful of French men and women living in New France were no match for the thousands of warriors the Five Nations of the Iroquois Confederacy could muster. And the Iroquois soon had firearms, supplied by the Dutch, depriving the French of the upper hand they had once enjoyed when it came to technology. For the moment, the Iroquois were merely a nuisance, but it was enough to create a climate of insecurity and disrupt the supply of furs along the St. Lawrence. When at last, in 1634, Champlain was able to open a second permanent post, it was at Trois-Rivières.

The project of establishing a settlement in Montreal was postponed until the situation improved. In 1636, Jean de

Lauson, manager of the Compagnie des Cent-Associés that controlled New France, used a frontman to get the company to grant him a seigneury that took in the entire island of Montreal. Under the seigneurial system, the seigneur was expected to grant lots to new settlers he would recruit, but Jean de Lauson had no intention of fulfilling those obligations and settling the island. It was sheer speculation: Lauson was well placed to see Montreal's potential.

CHAPTER 2

Ville-Marie
1642–1665

Champlain had dreamed of setting up a trading post at Montreal, but in 1642 a missionary settlement got there first. And so, although the city was most often called Montréal, it also came to be known as Ville-Marie. The beginnings were difficult, but *Montréalistes*, as they were known, stuck it out and gradually put down roots.

A mission

To understand the context in which Montreal was founded, we need to go back to France in the 1630s. Religion was back in favour; a wave of exaltation and a desire to spread the Catholic faith had washed over part of France's elite, affecting both the nobility and bourgeoisie. It spawned a host of new works, from religious orders and charities to missions. A secret society, the Company of the Blessed Sacrament (Compagnie du Saint-Sacrement), channelled part of this energy and brought together many of the kingdom's most influential figures. This was also a time when French Catholics were learning about missions in Canada, thanks in particular to *The Jesuit Relations*, chronicles of their time in New France.

This was the world of the man behind the Montreal project, Jérôme Le Royer de La Dauversière, a tax collector from

La Flèche in France. A fervent Catholic, he founded a number of religious and charitable organizations in his town and was also a member of the Company of the Blessed Sacrament. Around 1635, he first had the idea of founding a missionary settlement in Montreal. His project began to take shape in 1639 when he met Father Jean-Jacques Olier in Paris, a French priest who would go on to found the Sulpicians, and who was already nursing a similar idea. Together they managed to rally the rich and influential around their project, including the superior of the Company of the Blessed Sacrament, Gaston de Renty.

They set up the Société de Notre-Dame de Montréal to convert the Aboriginal peoples of New France. Their goal was to found a missionary settlement in Montreal where Aboriginals who had converted to Catholicism would live and farm alongside the French. The fur trade, still the main reason for many staying in Canada, was of no interest to them; their mission was religious. Their directors managed to raise a considerable amount of money to meet the needs of the colony and its inhabitants.

The Société de Notre-Dame purchased the seigneury of the island of Montreal that had previously belonged to Jean de Lauson and looked for someone to run the settlement. They picked the right man for the job in Paul de Chomedey de Maisonneuve, a gentleman with a military career behind him. They also brought on board Jeanne Mance, a woman with a project of her own, namely to found a hospital in Montreal, with the financial support of a rich benefactor, Madame de Bullion. Jeanne Mance became the settlement's bursar. Others were indentured servants—artisans, for the most part—who were recruited on three- to five-year contracts.

The Compagnie des Cent-Associés (Company of One Hundred Associates), which owned New France, granted the

Société de Notre-Dame a great deal of autonomy over its settlement in Montreal. It was able to name its own governor, Maisonneuve, who enjoyed a vast range of military and civilian powers, especially over judicial matters. It was also able to freely import the products it needed to Canada and had its own warehouse at Quebec.

Montreal's founding

The forty-person expedition set sail in 1641. There were three boats, but Maisonneuve's was damaged and delayed, not arriving until the end of the summer. It was too late in the year to set up the new settlement so the group spent the winter near Quebec, where it continued preparations, got used to the Canadian climate, and familiarized itself with techniques to survive the winter.

The governor of Quebec, Montmagny, deemed a settlement in Montreal risky, given attacks by the Iroquois and the small population of New France. He tried to get Maisonneuve to give up on the project—a "foolhardy undertaking," in his eyes—and to build a settlement on Île d'Orléans instead. But Maisonneuve stuck to his guns: he would build a settlement in Montreal, even if "all the trees on the island were to turn into just as many Iroquois." The autonomy granted to the Montreal colony also irritated the governor. In other words, even before the city was founded, there were already signs of legendary rivalry between what would go on to become Montreal and Quebec City.

In May 1642, accompanied by a small group from Quebec, including Governor Montmagny, Maisonneuve and his group set off up the river for Montreal. They arrived on May 17. The Jesuit Barthélemy Vimont said mass and gave a famous sermon in which he compared the new settlement to a mustard

MAISONNEUVE MONUMENT

Paul de Chomedey de Maisonneuve (1612-1676) was the founding governor of Montreal in 1642 and remained in that position until 1665. This monument to him, commissioned to sculptor Louis-Philippe Hébert and located at Place d'Armes in the heart of Old Montreal, was unveiled in 1895.

(Archives de la Ville de Montréal, BM42-G1106)

seed and predicted a bright future for it. Montreal had been founded.

Maisonneuve chose to settle on the spot later known as Pointe-à-Callière, the same site pinpointed by Champlain in 1611. The first year was devoted to building a fort and living quarters. An additional 12 settlers, sent by the Société de Notre-Dame, arrived at the end of summer 1642, meaning that fifty-odd men and women—mostly men—would spend a first winter in Montreal.

But Maisonneuve did not lose sight of his primary mission and tried to convince the Aboriginal people who passed through to come and make their home alongside the French. The project stood little chance against the harsh reality of war, however. The Iroquois had begun to control the fur routes along the St. Lawrence and Ottawa rivers. They systematically attacked rival nations, annihilating many of them, as was the case with the Hurons in 1649.

The founding of Montreal was a direct threat to the Iroquois. It took them a year to realize the new settlement existed, but once they did, they relentlessly spied on and harassed the Montréalistes, even managing to capture and kill a few of them. From that moment on, Ville-Marie was on the defensive; the dream of attracting Aboriginal peoples to the settlement evaporated since there was no way of guaranteeing their safety. The survival of the tiny colony was already hanging by a thread.

Montreal's history in the early years is therefore closely linked to its military heroics. The inhabitants survived by organizing their defences, keeping their wits about them whenever they dealt with the Iroquois, and making the most of lulls in the fighting. There were many tales of bravery among settlers convinced they were working for the glory of God (the religious ideals behind the settlement remained, even though the project of building a mission had stalled). And the charismatic Maisonneuve and Jeanne Mance helped keep the group together.

The war forced the Montréalistes to live inside the fort as much as possible, which curbed the development of agriculture. A few pieces of land were given to the settlers and some was cleared, but not much. In 1645, a hospital was built during a truce with the Iroquois, the Hôtel-Dieu that had drawn Jeanne Mance to the project. The building was not erected at Pointe-à-Callière—too vulnerable to flooding—but on the other side of the Petite rivière Saint-Pierre, where the city would later develop. Some settlers also began building homes for themselves on that side of the river.

Meanwhile, the population was stagnating. After initial efforts in 1641–1642, the Société de Notre-Dame sent few new settlers for the rest of the decade, and none at all in some years. Births were also scarce. New arrivals barely filled the void left by people leaving Montreal and those lost to war and other causes. Ten years after it was founded, Montreal still had no more than 50 people living there. Early results had not been encouraging, and in the early 1650s, the future appeared gloomy indeed for the handful of Montréalistes persisting with the project. A solution would have to be found.

Taking root

In 1651, Maisonneuve returned to France to recruit new settlers. He believed it was now or never for Montreal: if he failed to garner new recruits, the experiment would have to be brought to an end. Jeanne Mance suggested he use some of the funds earmarked for the Hôtel-Dieu, financial support that would prove decisive. But times were hard in France. The Montreal project was greeted less warmly than in 1641, although associates from the Société de Notre-Dame nevertheless managed to scrape together the money required to fund a new recruitment drive. In 1653, Maisonneuve at last returned with reinforcements: 95 new settlers, enough to triple the population of Ville-Marie in one swoop! The years that followed saw only a few immigrants arrive, but in 1659 one last push brought 91 more settlers. The colony could breathe again.

The recent wave of immigration had brought with it couples and single young women, who were quickly asked for their hand in marriage. It was enough to counterbalance what had until then been a surfeit of men. The next natural step was, of course, a spurt of births that, for the first time ever, gave a real boost to Montreal's population (estimated at 596 in 1663 by historian Marcel Trudel). From a tiny missionary settlement with an uncertain future, Montreal had blossomed into a permanent colony that was increasingly taking root.

Maisonneuve's presence as governor throughout these growing pains ensured some degree of continuity and stability. He administered the colony with a good dose of paternalism and managed to keep his little family together. Responsible for justice, he came down on misdemeanours, and as military commander, he surrounded himself with reliable officers like Lambert Closse. The other pillar of the colony was, of course, Jeanne Mance. She had also been there since the settlement's beginnings and, along with Maisonneuve, worked with French associates and donors.

The religious ideal remained a fundamental part of life in Ville-Marie. In the first few years of the settlement, Jesuit missionaries served the tiny colony, but as the population grew, there was a burgeoning need for a permanent parish clergy. In 1657, the first priests arrived from the Saint-Sulpice seminary in Paris and a parish was formed. From that moment, the Sulpicians went on to play an ever-growing role in the history of Montreal.

Another key institution was the Hôtel-Dieu set up by Jeanne Mance. The hospital, built in 1645 and then expanded, was, along with the fort, the biggest building in town. The first Hospitallers of St. Joseph, a women's religious order, arrived from La Flèche in France in 1659. They assisted Jeanne Mance and eventually took over from her.

The recruitment drive of 1653 brought a young woman to Montreal, Marguerite Bourgeoys, who wanted to devote herself to educating children. She opened her first school in an old barn in 1658. The following year, she brought over a handful of companions from France who would go on to form the Congregation of Notre Dame with her.

Montreal now had a network of schools and hospitals adapted to the needs of its population. The directors of the Société de Notre-Dame gave these institutions land in prime locations. Revenue generated by the land would be used to fund their work.

At the same time, the town itself was taking shape. In addition to the huge plots of land set aside for religious institutions, Maisonneuve also gave away more modest sites. A first line of homes popped up along Saint-Paul street; a strip along the shores of the St. Lawrence was set aside as common grounds, known as the *Commune*, where the *habitants* could let their animals graze.

One of the objectives of the Société de Notre-Dame was to set up an agricultural settlement. The first years did not make any progress on this front, but in the 1650s rural land extended further around the town as the population grew. From 1648, a first seigneurial mill meant wheat could be ground into flour, which became the main product of local agriculture.

Since the island of Montreal was a seigneury, Maisonneuve gave parcels of land to settlers prepared to clear them. In 1654 and 1655, he even gave them cash bonuses to take the land (although the bonuses had to be reimbursed, if ever the settlers left Montreal). This system was an effective way of keeping people in the country once their contracts with the Société de Notre-Dame had ended and who might otherwise have been tempted to return to France. Land given out in this way was right on the periphery of the area reserved for the town, but lots were smaller than those around Quebec to keep the *habitants* closer together and better protected in the event of an attack. As elsewhere in the St. Lawrence Valley, land was divided into long rectangular strips fronting on the St. Lawrence, Rivière Saint-Martin, and Petite rivière Saint-Pierre.

So what about the fur trade, the leading economic activity in Canada at the time? The Société de Notre-Dame had no direct role in the fur trade, but the *habitants* were interested in it. From 1645, when the Communauté des Habitants, which had a monopoly on trade in New France, was formed, Montréalistes had a voice within the organization. But their involvement in trade was limited since their Aboriginal allies were reluctant to bring their furs to Montreal because of the Iroquois, often preferring long portages inland to trade at Quebec or Tadoussac at the mouth of the Saguenay instead. The Iroquois eliminated or dispersed many tribes allied with the French, further complicating matters. Deliveries were possible during outbreaks of peace, however, which also provided an opportunity for the *habitants* to trade with the Aboriginals. Montreal's involvement in the fur trade really began in the 1650s, with a few merchants like Charles Le Moyne and Jacques Le Ber becoming rising stars.

Iroquois raids intensified starting in the late 1650s, which led to a new strategy: sending Frenchmen up into the *Pays d'en haut* to bring back furs from the nations around the Great Lakes. Radisson and Des Groseillers paved the way in 1660, returning to Montreal with a lucrative haul.

This was the background to the Battle of Long Sault in 1660. The young soldier, commander of the city garrison, Adam Dollard des Ormeaux, came up with a plan to attack the Iroquois along the Ottawa River on their way back from a hunting expedition. It may also have been his intention to ensure safe passage for Radisson and Des Groseillers, who were expected back soon. Dollard des Ormeaux left Montreal with 17 companions, taking up position at the Long Sault rapids along with a few Algonquins and some forty Hurons. But soon they came up against a group of Iroquois who were preparing to launch a major attack on New France. The Iroquois called for reinforcements posted at the mouth of the Richelieu River, and after several days of fighting, the French and the few Algonquins and Hurons who had remained loyal to them were defeated and killed. The battle nevertheless relieved the pressure exerted by the Iroquois that year.

At first wholly dependent on the Société de Notre-Dame for materials and supplies, the Montreal colony was beginning to generate economic activity of its own. A social structure was also taking shape. First, there was the group of *habitants*, the people who were no longer employed by the Société de Notre-Dame and who owned property in Montreal. They were fortunate enough to be able to trade with the Aboriginals and were the lifeblood of Montreal society. They included farmers, artisans, a small number of future merchants who came into their own later on, and a smattering of nobles. A new society like Montreal was a place of social and economic mobility for many of them. Then came the indentured servants who worked for the Société de Notre-Dame, the journeymen, tradesmen, and servants. They formed the largest group in 1663: historian Marcel Trudel estimates that two thirds of Montrealers worked for the other third.

Sweeping changes in France in 1663 altered the course of Montreal's history. The Company of One Hundred Associates stopped managing New France, which would now be governed by a more centralizing royal administration. The considerable autonomy Montreal had enjoyed since it had been founded was reduced. What's more, the Société de Notre-Dame, short on energy and resources, was dissolved and the seigneury of Montreal was transferred to the Saint-Sulpice seminary in Paris.

The new French administration, determined to come to the aid of its subjects who were being harassed by the Iroquois, sent troops in 1665. Their expeditions to Mohawk lands had little military success, but did bring about peace, to the great relief of Montrealers. That same year, Maisonneuve was somewhat cavalierly sent back to France by the king's representative without a word of explanation.

It was the end of an era, the end of Montreal's beginnings. Montreal now had roots, thanks to the efforts of the Société de Notre-Dame and the courage and tenacity of its inhabitants, in particular Maisonneuve and Jeanne Mance.

CHAPTER 3

The Heart of an Empire

For close to a century, Montreal was the beating heart
of a commercial and political empire that covered a large
portion of North America. It was at the head of a fur-trading
network whose needs drove the territorial expansion of New
France. And it also helped lead to the creation of a French
empire in North America, of which Montreal was a key hub.
This aspect of Montreal's development deserves a chapter to
itself. Other aspects of Montreal's history in the age of
New France are addressed in another chapter.

The fur trade and a widening sphere of influence

The French military intervention of 1665–1666 led to a period
of relative peace with the Iroquois and trade picked up again
in a big way. Middlemen, mainly from the Odawa nation,
hauled large loads of goods to Montreal, and the annual fur
fair every summer was a highlight of life in Montreal,
although it diminished in importance as a new system took
hold.

Over time, Montrealers got into the habit of organizing
their own trading expeditions, eliminating the need for
Aboriginal middlemen. At the start, these *coureurs des bois*
or woodsmen were illegal, but the government legalized—and
controlled—the new system in 1681. Trading permits were

now required for expeditions to the *Pays d'en haut*. Needless to say, keeping a close eye on such a vast area was difficult, and some traders continued to operate illegally.

Expeditions were usually organized by merchants associated with voyageurs who worked the canoes. Merchants outfitted the expedition and provided the goods to be exchanged, while voyageurs headed west to trade and bring furs back to Montreal. Profits were shared between both parties. Voyageurs took on hired hands to transport the goods.

Demand led to the overexploitation of fur-bearing animals and the gradual exhaustion of stocks. This meant that voyageurs had to travel further and further to find areas that had been less exploited. This in turn encouraged exploration of the continent and widened the sphere of influence dominated by Montreal. Montreal's footprint extended as far as the Great Lakes as of 1679, when Daniel Duluth reached the far end of Lake Superior, hence the name of the American city of Duluth. Then came expansion to the south: in 1673 Jolliet and Marquette reached the Mississippi, in 1682 La Salle made it to the mouth of the Mississippi, and in 1699 Montreal's Pierre Le Moyne d'Iberville founded Louisiana. (His own brother, Jean-Baptiste Le Moyne de Bienville, also a Montrealer, would later be the founder of New Orleans. Moreover, the layout of what is now the French Quarter of New Orleans was inspired by the layout of Montreal.) The following century, expansion spread west: between 1731 and 1743 La Vérendrye and his sons explored all the south of what are now the Canadian Prairies and the north of the Great Plains on the other side of the current Canada-U.S. border.

Expansion so far from the Montreal base soon required permanent trading posts to be set up in the west, where voyageurs would spend the winter with the local inhabitants. These posts often doubled as forts—some with a garrison— that ensured the political and military control of the region in the name of the king of France. The biggest forts were at Detroit, at the entrance to Lake Erie, and at Michilimakinac, where Lake Huron meets Lake Michigan. Western expansion was also justified by competition from English merchants plying their trade both to the south (the New York colony) and to the north (the Hudson's Bay Company). The English sold certain supplies for less and sometimes paid more for furs. Both the Aboriginals and the French were therefore tempted to go for the better deal. Like trading permits, contraband was difficult to control.

Montreal merchants also met with internal competition. There was, of course, competition among themselves, but it also came from the colony's administrators at Quebec, who traded in secret, as well as the officers in charge of the garrisons out west, who traded to cover their expenses. If merchants were to survive, they had to join forces with the competition. Growing numbers of people involved in trading also contributed to the colony's expansion.

The fur trade was therefore a complex world, where stakeholders and alliances could change depending on who was governor at Quebec. In the 1690s and 1700s, trade was hindered by overproduction of beaver pelts, which sparked a real crisis. The colony's administrators sought to resolve this problem by reducing trade, which led merchants to look for other types of fur.

Montreal merchants could not be expected to make a fortune in such conditions. Some of them became rich through trade, but their fortunes were subject to the vagaries of war, competition, and the market. In any event, Montreal remained the organizing force behind the fur trade and the gateway to the west. All the leading merchants settled in the town, most voyageurs and hired labourers came from the Montreal area, and trading expeditions were organized and equipped in

Montreal. Although small in stature, Montreal was already a nerve centre whose influence could be felt thousands of kilometres away.

All this activity did not lead to the growth of Montreal by itself, however, since it required no real labour in the town. Aboriginals were the providers, while more than a thousand Frenchmen—or *Canadiens* as they were known—mainly from Montreal, worked out west in the last decades of New France, many of them for long spells. In Montreal, a handful of merchants, with the help of a few clerks and servants, were enough to manage businesses and handle goods. A few artisans made tools and clothing to be traded with the Aboriginals, but most products were imported from France. Profits from trade were invested in building new homes, warehouses, and stores in Montreal or were spent on services. Once the system was up and running, the number of people working in this sector in the town remained fairly stable.

The fur trade nevertheless remained Montreal's principal economic activity and source of income. According to historian Louise Dechêne, one third of the working population depended on the fur trade, directly or indirectly. It was a source of fascination for many Montrealers who hoped to cash in on the opportunities it offered, one way or another. The lure of the west remained hard to resist, and the spirit of adventure left its mark on Montreal's way of thinking. Young people, often from farming families, left the Montreal area in droves to work out west for a season or two as hired labourers before settling down on their land and starting a family.

France's North American Empire

Though westward expansion was born of commercial needs, it also became part of France's political and military strategy, namely creating a French-speaking domain in North America that would counterbalance the expansionism of England and its colonies. All new lands explored were officially claimed in the name of the king of France and, by the start of the eighteenth century, France's North American Empire stretched from Acadia to Louisiana, spanning much of the continent and encircling the English colonies. Montreal now played a pivotal role as a gateway to the west.

The success of the strategy required an alliance with the Aboriginal nations, crucial commercial partners who were also a military power that the French chose to join forces with. At the end of the seventeenth century, the weak link in this policy remained the Iroquois, partners of the English. Hostilities resumed in the 1680s, leading to a French military expedition against the Seneca people in 1687. In 1689, an Iroquois war party attacked Lachine, killing some of the villagers and taking others prisoner. The Lachine massacre plunged Montreal into turmoil. Iroquois raids would only intensify in the area over the years to come.

Governor Frontenac replied by organizing punitive raids on villages in the English colonies, then by undertaking a military expedition against Iroquois villages in 1696. This brought an end to the conflict, but Frontenac wanted a lasting peace. His successor, Louis-Hector de Callière, would continue the project and in 1701 managed to get some 40 Aboriginal nations from among their traditional allies and the Iroquois Five Nations to sign the Great Peace or Grand Settlement of Montreal, both among themselves and with France. The far-reaching event saw over a thousand Aboriginal delegates travel to Montreal from afar to take part in the discussions and the impressive rituals surrounding the negotiations. The Treaty of 1701 became the cornerstone of the strategic alliance with the Aboriginals. The Iroquois officially

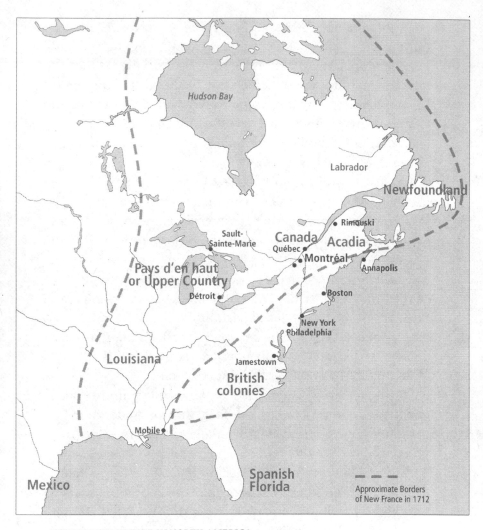

Hudson Bay

Labrador

Newfoundland

Rimouski

Sault-
Sainte-Marie   Canada   Acadia
                    Québec
Pays d'en haut   Montréal
or Upper Country   Annapolis

Détroit   Boston

                              New York
                          Philadelphia

Louisiana   Jamestown

                   British
                   colonies

        Mobile

Mexico   Spanish
                   Florida   – – – –
                                      Approximate Borders
                                      of New France in 1712

THE FRENCH EMPIRE IN NORTH AMERICA

This map shows the maximum extension of New France around 1712. The following year, the Treaty of Utrecht would mark the first step in the dismantling of that empire, completed by the Treaty of Paris in 1763. Montreal occupied a commanding position within this empire.

(Les éditions du Septentrion)

THE TREATY OF 1701

The Great Peace or Grand Settlement of Montreal, in 1701, was signed by the leaders of some 40 Indian nations. Their signatures represent the totems symbolizing their names.

(Archives nationales de France, fonds des Colonies)

remained neutral in conflicts between the English and the French and would never again threaten Montreal. A major page in the town's history had been turned.

From this point on, it was the struggle between the English and the American colonies that would be the focus of military attention. Between 1689 and 1763, four major wars broke out in Europe, pitting France against England. These wars had repercussions in North America, where the colonies also had their reasons for fighting with each other. The history of each conflict goes beyond the scope of this book, but suffice it to say that Montreal was involved on many levels. In 1690 and 1711, it was the target of two Anglo-American expeditions intending to lead an invasion via the Richelieu River Valley, but both turned back before reaching Montreal.

Montrealers took part in the military effort. Many noblemen were officers for the French troops, while the bourgeoisie and *habitants* joined the Canadian militia. Militiamen in particular were used in the raids against the English colonies.

No one epitomizes Montreal's involvement in military efforts and France's expansionist strategy in North America more than Pierre Le Moyne d'Iberville, the best-known son of merchant Charles Le Moyne. From 1686 to 1697, he took part in many campaigns against English Hudson's Bay settlements and helped make a French presence possible there, all while reaping the benefits of the fur trade. In 1690, he took part in one of the raids organized by Frontenac against the English colonies at Corlaer in what is now upstate New York. Then, in 1696, he led a French expedition that first went on a campaign in Acadia, then captured some of the English posts in Newfoundland as far east as St. John's, this time profiting from the cod trade. Three years later, he founded Louisiana, where he set up a first French fort. He died in Havana in 1706, on an expedition against the English West Indies. D'Iberville is a prime example of the ties between commercial and strategic considerations in French expansion in North America. He was also a testament to Montrealers' ability to adapt to the North American environment and their continental vision.

The governors of Montreal also had an important role to play since, in addition to ensuring the town's defences, they tended to be responsible for organizing military expeditions across the continent. Some went on to have brilliant careers in the colony. Louis-Hector de Callière, for instance, who held the post from 1684 to 1698, was Governor General of Canada from 1698 until his death in 1703. Philippe de Rigaud de Vaudreuil, his successor as governor of Montreal in 1699, also took over the role of Governor General from 1703 to 1725 and founded a veritable dynasty, with his son Pierre occupying the colony's highest post from 1755 to 1760 and another of his sons, François-Pierre, becoming governor of Montreal in 1757. For his part, Claude de Ramezay stands out for the length of his term as governor of Montreal (1704–1724) and had one of the town's grandest houses built for himself.

The many wars that punctuated the first half of the eighteenth century led the French government to bolster the colony's military defences. They had a number of forts built, each defended by a garrison, in the Great Lakes region, in the Mississippi region, at Louisbourg on Cape Breton Island, along the Richelieu, and in the Ohio Valley. In Montreal itself, officers and soldiers from the *Troupes de la Marine,* the equivalent of modern-day marines, had been part of daily life since 1683. Their numbers swelled in times of war, and the buildup towards expeditions across the continent from Montreal added to the excitement. At the start, France supplied the troops, but from the eighteenth century onward Canada's merchants and farmers took over the role of provider. Procurement for the troops and the soldiers' pay stimulated the local economy and had money circulate around the town.

Military considerations were also behind the authorities' decision to fortify the town. Louis-Hector de Callière, then governor of Montreal, had a wooden stockade put up between 1687 and 1689 in order to protect the town from the Iroquois. In the following century, the stockade was replaced by a stone wall, this time designed to keep English attacks at bay. The engineer Chaussegros de Léry built the wall between 1717 and 1744.

But the balance of power was to shift against Canada in the long term. England dominated the seas and England's colonies were much more densely populated than France's. The Seven Years' War from 1756 to 1763 saw Anglo-American troops deliver the death blow to New France. The colony's fate played out at the Battle of the Plains of Abraham in 1759, and Quebec fell into the hands of the invading troops. In the summer of 1760, three British armies marched on Montreal, one from the west down the St. Lawrence, one from the south going down the Richelieu, and another from the east coming up the St. Lawrence. Governor Vaudreuil, who had withdrawn to Montreal, saw that resistance was futile and capitulated on September 8, 1760. It marked the end of the French North American Empire. The British Conquest would have major consequences for Montreal, and we will explore them in Chapter 5.

CHAPTER 4

A Small French Town
1665–1760

After our brief look at the fur trade and French expansion in North America, time now to return to the town and its development. Montreal's political and administrative reorganization from 1663 to 1665 turned a new page in its history: the remote settlement was taking on the trappings of an urban centre. Its institutions and general look and feel were just like those of a small town in the depths of the French countryside. The name "Ville-Marie" quickly fell by the wayside: despite a strong religious presence, the missionary ideal behind the settlement had given way to commercial interests. So what was Montreal like in the late seventeenth and eighteenth centuries? And the people who lived there?

The town's development

Montreal had a population of some 600 people in 1663 and twice as many by the turn of the century. The number of people who lived there passed the 3,000 mark around 1731 and 4,000 in 1754. Growth rate picked up a little during the peace that followed the Treaty of Utrecht in 1713, but generally lagged behind the rest of Canada.

Between 1663 and 1760, the countryside of the St. Lawrence Valley saw the strongest population growth. Peace with the

Iroquois helped agriculture develop around Montreal. Having for years been concentrated close to the town, it gradually extended to the rest of the island, spilling over to Île Jésus or Jesus island (now the city of Laval) and the north and south shores.

On the island of Montreal, as elsewhere in the colony, rural settlements were divided into strips of long lots or ribbon farms, known as *côtes* on the island and *rangs* in other areas. A *côte* was a group of plots of land and homes, arranged one beside the other along the St. Lawrence or, inland, along a road of the same name as the *côte*. The road that led to each *côte* was known as a *montée*, even if the land was flat, as in Saint-Laurent. Long *côtes* were the basic social unit in the Montreal countryside, which boasted around thirty of them in 1731. Even though the Church created rural parishes, the *côtes* were still more common.

As well as being the place where the fur trade was organized, Montreal became a hub for farming. This gave rise to a number of trades that, although modest at the start, grew throughout the eighteenth century. Agricultural surpluses sustained the town and began to be sent to markets at Quebec and Louisbourg. Montreal merchants took part in the business and sold farmers imported products they could not make themselves. This developed into a lucrative business, although curbed by the countryside's sparse population (in the year of the Conquest in 1760, all of Canada still had no more than 60,000 inhabitants of French origin, too few to support a diversified economy).

Artisanal production that developed in Montreal was mostly limited to local needs—construction, baking, sewing, tanning, shoe-repairs, and furniture making, along with stores for smiths, armourers, and coopers—although it was boosted by the demands of war.

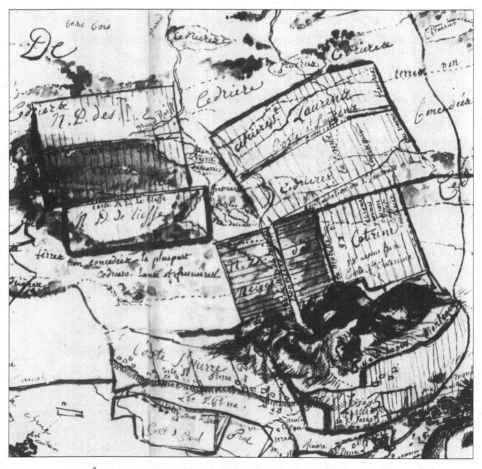

THE *CÔTES*: A VITAL PART OF RURAL LIFE IN MONTREAL

This segment of a 1702 map shows some of the earlier inland *côtes* on the island of Montreal. The subdivision of rural land in strips of narrow rectangular farms linked by a common road is an obvious feature here. As can be seen, Montreal has maintained both the names of those subdivisions and some of the roads.

(Archives de la Ville de Montréal, VM66-S1P025)

This explains why, under the French regime, Montreal remained a small town. But it was nonetheless a town, its space organized differently than the countryside. In 1672, Dollier de Casson, the superior of the Sulpicians, sought to impose some order on Montreal by marking out its streets. There were two main east-west thoroughfares—Saint-Paul and Notre-Dame—and a number of side streets. Most of these streets existed only on paper, but they were gradually opened in the decades to come, which means that, even today, a modern map of Old Montreal looks very much like a map from 1672. The town itself occupied a clearly defined area and was surrounded by fortifications from 1687 on. Toward 1730, the first suburbs, called *faubourgs*, began to spring up outside the wall, along the main thoroughfares.

For many years, the town's homes and main buildings were made from wood and often fell prey to fires, the scourge of pre-industrial towns. Montreal was not spared its share of blazes, which destroyed homes by the dozen, first in 1721 and 1734, then after the Conquest in 1765 and 1768. Various intendants decreed that new buildings within the town limits be made from stone, but many wooden buildings remained at the end of the French regime. In an effort to stop the flames spreading, firewalls went up, peeking out over the roofs of the houses, where sheet metal or slate had replaced cedar shingles.

More modest homes had only one floor with an attic, but new stone homes built in the eighteenth century tended to have an extra floor. They had a gable roof and sometimes skylights. The basements of bigger buildings—those belonging to merchants, for instance—had vaults for storing goods. One such building was the former residence of Governor Claude de Ramezay, rebuilt in 1756 by the Compagnie des Indes, which used it as a store and warehouse. In the suburbs, most buildings were made from wood, a distinction that revealed a difference in social class since only the rich could afford stone homes. Gradually Montrealers from modest backgrounds set up home in the suburbs, increasingly leaving the town itself to the elites.

The town was also home to the Hôtel-Dieu hospital, the seminary, and convents belonging to other religious orders, all with their own gardens. In the upper town, right at the centre of Rue Notre-Dame, stood the parish church, built in 1672, with a bell tower that dominated the skyline. Following the example of France's small towns, Montreal had public squares of its own. Near the port, Place du Marché, the public marketplace, was the liveliest of the lot. That was where farmers gathered to sell their goods to the townspeople and where crowds formed to watch the punishments reserved for the condemned. The remains of the houses that ran alongside the square can still be seen today at the Pointe-à-Callière museum. A second square stood in the shadow of the church and would soon be surrounded by homes: Place d'Armes.

There was no shortage of space in this little French town, and population was much less dense than in European centres of comparable size. Montrealers were not forced to live cheek by jowl, and the suburbs provided an outlet for expansion.

A distinct society

Montreal society was well organized. It was different in many ways to the population of Quebec, a trait that had been visible since its founding. After 1663, Montreal did lose some of the autonomy that had characterized its first 20 years of existence. The governor of Montreal became more closely bound to the authority of the governor general of New France and his role became a purely military one. The intendant, based at Quebec,

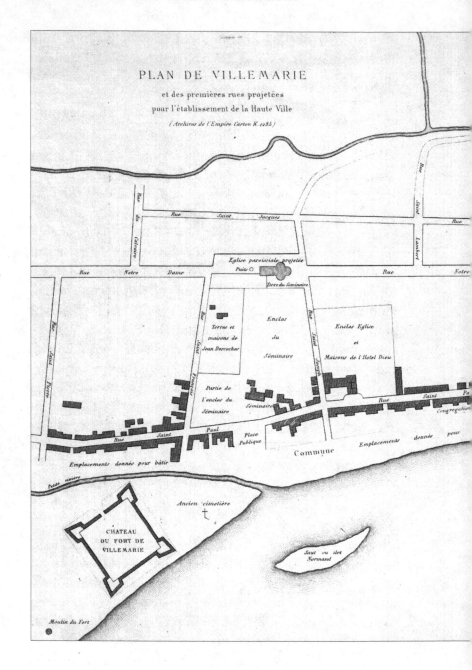

PLAN DE VILLEMARIE

et des premières rues projetées

pour l'établissement de la Haute Ville

(Archives de l'Empire Carton K.1285)

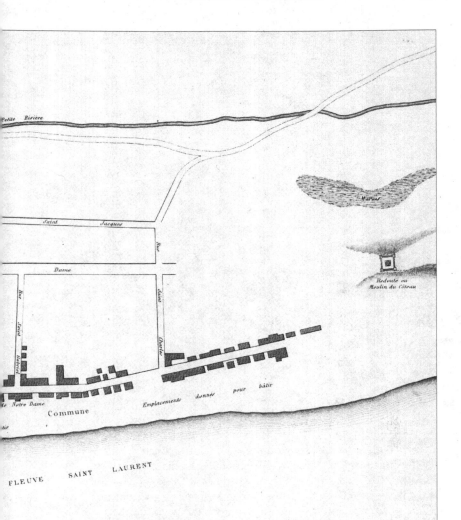

MONTREAL IN 1685

Montreal was still a small town some 43 years after it was founded. Whereas the fort still occupied its birthplace, most of the buildings were now located along Saint-Paul street. The marketplace (Place Publique) was the commercial nexus, while the newly built church was located in the middle of Notre-Dame street.

(Archives de la Ville de Montréal, BM5-3_41_C26-Inv45)

CHÂTEAU RAMEZAY

One of the oldest buildings still standing in Montreal, Château Ramezay was erected in 1756 for the Compagnie des Indes, on the site of the former house (1705) of local governor Claude de Ramezay. The tower on the left was added in 1903. After the British Conquest, it housed government services and even invading American troops in 1775-76 during the revolution. It became a historical museum in 1895.

(Archives de la Ville de Montréal, VM94Z686-1)

took over responsibility for civilian matters, with a sub-delegate in Montreal. In many areas, royal justice replaced seigneurial justice. This loss of autonomy did not sit well with Montrealers, who had a tendency to resist orders sent from afar.

Religious institutions also lost some of the autonomy they had previously enjoyed. The nomination of a first bishop at Quebec in 1658, Monseigneur de Laval, was a source of tension, although Montreal institutions did remain distinct from the religious orders at Quebec. The biggest organization in Montreal was the Saint-Sulpice seminary, at once the island's seigneur and the entity responsible for the parish ministry. The seminary had a significant influence on the town's development. Its responsibilities and seigneurial revenues made it an economic powerhouse, while it was also responsible for elementary schools for boys and helped the town's religious works and charities in countless ways.

The Hospitallers of St. Joseph, originally from La Flèche in France, succeeded Jeanne Mance as managers of the Hôtel-Dieu. Elementary education, both in the town and the surrounding countryside, was provided by the Congregation of Notre Dame. The congregation was founded by Marguerite Bourgeoys and went on to become the biggest religious order in New France.

François Charon de La Barre founded the Frères hospitaliers de la Croix et de Saint-Joseph (the Hospitaller Brothers of the Cross and St. Joseph) and had the Hôpital général or general hospital built from 1692 to 1694. Despite its name, the hospital did not provide medical care, instead focusing on social services and providing shelter to the poor, the elderly, and the mentally ill. The religious order also taught boys for a time but it disappeared in 1747 and was replaced at the Hôpital général by the Sisters of Charity, more commonly known as the Grey Nuns. This community was established in

1737 by Marie-Marguerite Dufrost de Lajemmerais, widow of François d'Youville, with the aim of helping the poor.

Montreal had formed and left its mark on each of these orders, most of whose members were born in Canada. The sole exception was the Seminary—an association of secular priests rather than a true religious order—which recruited only in France and kept close ties with its mother house in Paris. The bishops of New France attempted on several occasions to merge the religious orders of Montreal with those of Quebec, but resistance proved too strong and Montreal retained its distinct identity.

At the end of the seventeenth century, two major religious orders joined the group. The Jesuits returned to Montreal after a hiatus that had lasted several decades. They set up home in the east of the town, while the *Récollets*, or Recollects, built their convent in the far west.

With so many orders in the city, the Church was front and centre in Montreal life. Its institutions were an economic mainstay, with buildings to be constructed, land to be farmed, and revenue to be invested. The Church's impact on local employment was considerable, its hold over the town itself, striking.

The military aristocracy continued to be present around town and its members made a name for themselves by obtaining commissions as officers in the *Troupes de la Marine*. A handful of administrative and justice officers rounded out this elite. For their part, merchants still enjoyed a privileged status and monopolized churchwarden positions. As the only civilians living in the town able to amass significant capital, they held more property than the average Montrealer, were waited on by servants, and owned slaves (most often enslaved Aboriginals from the Pawnee people in Western Canada, and sometimes Africans).

Artisans and innkeepers were able to amass some capital and employ apprentices or servants. Their lives remained fairly modest, however, given the dearth of economic activity in the colony. *Habitants*—a term increasingly used to designate farmers—had left town to settle on land in the neighbouring countryside, where people lived frugally.

The town had a good number of day labourers, who eked out a living in construction and transport. It was also a permanent home to soldiers, who spent most of their days drinking, gambling in taverns, and cavorting with prostitutes. They were the town's biggest source of crime and disorder.

In short, Montreal had a social hierarchy based on birth, trade, and money. The fur trade continued to be a way for people to get rich and even climb the social ladder. The call of the west and military expeditions led to frequent comings and goings and made Montreal feel like a frontier town: many of its men were constantly elsewhere, off in search of adventure, seeking fame and fortune.

From the days of New France, many observers have stressed the differences in thinking between Montreal and Quebec City. In 1749, for example, Swedish traveller Pehr Kalm wrote that Quebec women were more preoccupied with their appearance whereas those in Montreal were more devoted to their housework. The differences were no doubt amplified by the constant rivalry between the towns, their elites, and their citizens. In other words, although its institutions and urban planning gave Montreal the look and feel of a typical French town, its growing role on the continent and the way of thinking of the people who lived there were already making it an increasingly North American town.

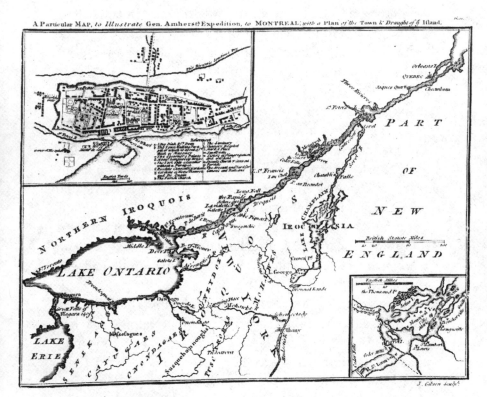

AMHERST'S MONTREAL

This map shows the geographical settings of General Amherst's expedition in 1760. In the inset, the city of Montreal is mapped with its walls and the built-up area within.

(Les éditions du Septentrion)

CHAPTER 5

Conquered
1760–1800

For the people of French origin living in Canada, the Conquest of 1760 had major consequences, the effects of which can still be felt today. It saw control of the country move into English hands and kicked off a new period of colonization that, in the long term, would lead to the original inhabitants becoming the minority. The first years of the British regime turned life in Montreal on its head, even though continuity with the French regime was significant in some areas.

Growth of the fur trade

In particular, Montreal retained its role as the hub of the fur trade until that trade disappeared from the city altogether in 1821.

The fur trade was seriously disrupted by the Seven Years' War (1756-1763), which is known in Quebec as *La guerre de la Conquête* and in the United States as the French and Indian War. The war in fact began in 1754 in North America but ended in 1760 when the Anglo-American troops took Montreal. Trade picked up again, however, after 1760, although the context had changed, as historian José Igartua has shown. The original Canadian merchants, cut off from their traditional ties with French suppliers, managed to obtain stock from the British. But competition had grown. The new people in power decreed freedom of trade, at a stroke rendering the trade permit system obsolete. Many newcomers, mainly British and American, set out in search of furs, sometimes with Canadian voyageurs, often going against traditional trade flows. Canadian merchants lost ground, disadvantaged because they had access neither to transportation contracts to the garrisons out west, nor to the system of patronage, which were reserved for the British. Many of them also lost a fortune because they held French paper money, never fully redeemed by the French crown after the Treaty of Paris. British merchants also found it easier to gather together the fairly considerable funds required for big westward expeditions. In the space of a few years, Canadian merchants found themselves being squeezed out by merchants from elsewhere, particularly Scots who had settled in Montreal.

But it wasn't all smooth sailing for the Scots either. Competition was fierce, and many fell by the wayside. After a few years, the likes of Frobisher, Henry, McGill, and McTavish were among the front-runners, becoming the beaver barons. Most of them had lived out west and had mastered the ins and outs of the trade.

Realizing that unfettered competition increases expenses and reduces profits, they looked to join forces, founding the North West Company in 1779. Over the years, most Montreal merchants joined the company, along with traders who spent the winter out west. The company set up a single network of trading posts and improved the transportation system, offering stiffer resistance to competition from the Hudson's Bay Company.

As under the French regime, Montrealers scoured the continent in the quest for new land and furs. Alexander Mackenzie, for example, explored the river that now bears his name, reaching the Arctic Ocean in 1789 before crossing the Rocky Mountains and hitting the Pacific in 1793.

At the start of the nineteenth century, the North West Company dominated the fur trade in British North America. It set up a dense network of trading posts that stretched all the way to the Pacific. Montreal pulled the strings, with merchants setting out from the town and furs passing through there en route to Great Britain. The company's main partners grew very rich indeed and dominated Montreal society. In 1785, they began to meet regularly in the winter to feast at the Beaver Club.

Some Montreal merchants did not belong to the association behind the North West Company and competed with it. They formed the XY Company in 1797, but after a few years of costly opposition, the North West Company swallowed up its rival in 1804.

The rudest competition came from the Hudson's Bay Company, however, which enjoyed lower transportation costs. After long being content with waiting for the Aboriginals at its posts on the shores of Hudson Bay, the company changed tack and decided it would also move inland. Hudson's Bay Company posts were soon popping up all over the west, alongside North West Company posts. Competition grew keener and prices rose, a costly undertaking for both companies. The two companies started negotiating and then merged in 1821 in favour of the Hudson's Bay Company.

The North West Company disappeared, and Hudson Bay was now the focus of the fur trade. Montreal thereby lost the trading empire that had been its raison d'être for over a century and a half. It would be decades before its business elite would again set foot on the Canadian Prairies, this time in the very different context of settlers moving in with the railroad.

Uncertain times

But let's shift our focus back to the town itself. From 1760 to 1764, Montreal was occupied by Anglo-American troops until a civilian government was set up. It was again occupied during the American War of Independence, this time for a few months by an American army in 1775–1776. Aside from this brief interlude, the town was home to a British garrison for close to a century, first in the east end of Montreal, then on Île Sainte-Hélène. But Montreal was no longer the key military post it had been for New France.

The most striking change brought about by the Conquest was the takeover of the economy by a handful of English, Scottish, and American merchants who had arrived on the army's coattails. Though few in number, these merchants were looking to play a key role in running the new British colony. They were against Catholics having access to official posts and called for English laws to be applied. The Royal Proclamation of 1763 satisfied them for the most part. Administrative posts were denied to Catholics unless they renounced their faith. Canada's elites put pressure on Great Britain to change this policy that barred them from public life, in turn winning their cause with the Quebec Act of 1774. Catholics were henceforth on an equal footing with Protestants and French civil law applied in the Province of Quebec, which then included what is now southern Ontario and part of the future U.S. territory.

Montreal's British merchants clamoured for a legislative assembly to be created, as in the other English colonies. Some were even sympathetic to the demands of the American colonies and would take their side during the American War of Independence and the occupation of Montreal in 1775–1776. The Americans tried to make Canadians more aware of their ideas while they occupied the town, but to no avail. This was the backdrop to the arrival from Philadelphia, and before that from France, of Fleury Mesplet, Montreal's first printer. Mesplet stayed in Montreal after the invading troops had left and in 1778 founded *La Gazette littéraire*, the town's first newspaper and ancestor of *The Montreal Gazette*.

The decades that followed the Conquest were, for Montreal as in the rest of the country, uncertain, characterized by intense struggles between British merchants and Canadian elites and marked by the American Revolution—familiar themes in the history of Canada.

In Montreal, the arrogance of British businessmen and their contempt for Canadians were a source of tension. For their part, the Canadian elites—particularly the religious authorities—displayed their loyalty to the British crown and sought support from the governor to counter the merchants' policies.

Since they were no more than a minority, the British had to adapt to life in the town. They had to use French as they went about their day-to-day business with locals; many married Canadians; fur traders, at least at the start, teamed up with Canadian voyageurs who knew all about the fur trade from their time out west and also were skilled at negotiating with the Aboriginal peoples. In other words, the elites did intermingle to a certain extent, even though they remained distinct in many ways. In the other echelons of society—among the artisans, day labourers, and *habitants*—not much changed and the population of Montreal was far and away of French origin.

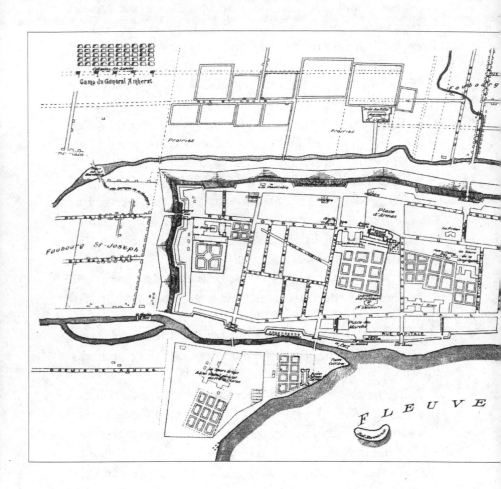

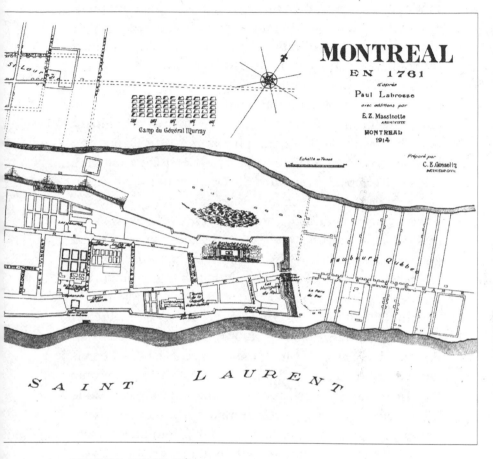

MONTREAL AROUND 1760

This redrawn version of an older map shows the location of generals Murray's and Amherst's troops at the time of the British Conquest. Within the walled city, the street grid and the largest gardens are visible, as well as the layout of the main surrounding suburbs.

(Archives de la Ville de Montréal, VM66-S2P006)

The seigneurial regime was maintained after the Conquest. Catholic institutions were one of the driving forces behind continuity and the Church managed to maintain its positions. The Saint-Sulpice seminary was given the seigneury of Montreal by the organization's seminary in Paris. Although the transaction was not immediately acknowledged by the British authorities, leaving the Sulpicians somewhat uncertain for a time, their rights were confirmed in the longer term, thus ensuring the seminary's financial security. The seminary remained at the head of the parish of Notre Dame, the Hospitallers continued their work at the Hôtel-Dieu, the Grey Nuns at the Hôpital général, and the sisters of the Congregation of Notre Dame in the schools. The British government did, however, ban male religious orders from recruiting new members, which meant that after a few decades the Jesuits and Récollets died out when their last member passed away.

The look and feel of the town did not change much in the decades that followed the Conquest. The British had homes built in the traditional Montreal style, a legacy of the French regime. In outward appearance, Montreal remained a small French town. The overhaul of the town centre, begun previously after fires, continued. The centre increasingly became the place where the business elite lived, building solid stone homes often bigger than those that had preceded them. Increasing numbers of artisans and day labourers moved to suburbs that, in the late 1700s, were home to more Montrealers than the town inside the walls. In 1792, these suburbs were included within Montreal's official limits.

The town was now governed differently: justices of the peace replaced the intendant and his representatives. Chosen by the colonial administration, these magistrates were drawn from the ranks of local elites. At first, they were mostly British, but French-speaking *Canadiens* became much more numerous after the Quebec Act of 1774. The magistrates were responsible for issuing rules concerning public works, construction, markets, local policing, and more—rules not much different to those previously laid down by the intendants in New France.

Towards the end of the eighteenth century, Montreal resembled a typical pre-industrial town, both in physical appearance and social structure, with the fur trade still the predominant activity. But major changes were afoot in the final few decades of the century, turning a new page on Montreal's history.

CHAPTER 6

A Gateway City
for the British Empire
1800–1850

For the first half of the nineteenth century, Montreal underwent a surprising series of changes. Growth surpassed previous levels, and new business activity took over from the fur trade, thereby transforming the city's economy. The population, which had swelled, was now composed of a majority of English speakers. The area the town covered was growing and needed to be managed in new ways.

A commercial metropolis

The transformations Montreal was undergoing can be explained first and foremost by mass immigration to Canada. The movement began after the American War of Independence when thousands of Loyalists moved north of the border, mainly to Ontario, which they began to colonize. And it increased in tempo after 1815 with the end of the Napoleonic Wars and Ireland's economic woes causing an unprecedented wave of migrants to leave the British Isles.

At the same time, the French-Canadian population was growing rapidly, thanks to a sky-high birth rate. The country-side of the plains around Montreal was populated in a matter of decades, skipping ahead of the population on the lands around Quebec City.

Whereas Montreal's small rural population had curbed the town's development in New France, the situation was now reversed. Montreal found itself at the heart of a rapidly expanding hinterland, which encompassed the vast plains surrounding it and, above all, Ontario, to which it was the main gateway. All these new farmers were in need of new products and were looking to sell their crop surpluses. Montreal would be the main broker in these exchanges.

The town found itself at the head of a much more diversified business that had considerable economic repercussions. It exported produce—mainly wheat—to Britain and imported a host of manufactured goods. This new situation also spurred local manufacturers. Ships were built in Montreal and equipment manufactured to meet business needs. Shoes were made there, along with hardware items and the other products that gradually replaced imports and were distributed across the countryside using networks set up by Montreal merchants. The town's increased population even created more work for a slew of small producers. Items continued to be made in artisans' workshops for the most part, but bigger factories like John Molson's brewery were beginning to emerge.

Such a boom in activity boosted the construction and retail sectors, needless to say, but the services sector swelled too. Transportation required a bigger labour force, and inns were popping up all over town—newspapers too. More servants were needed as well. In these circumstances, the loss of the fur trade in 1821 was not devastating, such was the extent to which Montreal's economy had diversified in past decades.

But the transportation system had to be reorganized if new businesses in Montreal were to operate efficiently. Birch bark canoes had been well suited to the fur trade, but proved hopeless for meeting the demands of trade on a much larger scale. And so Montreal merchants had boats built and founded shipping companies to manage transportation between Montreal and Ontario and between Montreal and Quebec City. In 1809, John Molson launched *Accommodation*, the first steamship on the St. Lawrence, which shuttled back and forth between Montreal and Quebec City. Businessmen also got the government to set up a system of canals on the St. Lawrence, allowing their ships to bypass numerous rapids. The Lachine Canal, a project that had been dreamt up by the Sulpicians in the days of New France, at last became a reality in 1825 and would be expanded in the 1840s. Other canals were added along the St. Lawrence, all the way to the Great Lakes.

The port also required some work. The muddy shoreline that stretched out before the town meant that ships had to weigh anchor off Montreal and unload their goods using smaller craft. Merchants wanted wharves and demanded a permanent organization be created to develop them. Their wish was granted when the Montreal Harbour Commission was set up in 1830, with commercial interests well represented. The commission set to work immediately and the wharves were built.

Starting in the 1830s, the businessmen of Montreal also developed an interest in a new means of transport: the train. In 1836, they built the first railway in Canada, linking Laprairie to Saint-Jean on the south shore and hastening communications with the United States, and were involved in many other railway projects throughout the following decade.

Masters of transportation, Montreal's businessmen honed their control over the economy by setting up a trading network that encompassed everyone, from the importers/exporters in Montreal to the smaller merchants in the countryside, not to mention the regional wholesalers in between. It was backed by credit provided by businesses in Great Britain. Given the number of financial transactions, the businessmen soon set up their own banks, starting with the first bank in Canada, the Bank of Montreal, founded in 1817.

All these changes saw Montreal replace Quebec City as the country's largest and leading city from the 1830s. It was now the economic powerhouse of Canada and an important economic link in the British Empire, but despite its position of dominance, Montreal remained sorely dependent on the United Kingdom and its businesses.

A new population

Economic expansion brought with it a population boom that outpaced the rest of the country. In the second half of the eighteenth century, Montreal's population doubled, before increasing sixfold over the next half century. A town of some 9,000 souls around 1800, it was home to 23,000 in 1825 and 58,000 in 1852. By then the most populous city in Canada, it would hold on to this title for the next century and a half.

Immigration played a key role in this growth. The 1825 census already revealed that one third of Montrealers had been born abroad and, by the following census in 1831, one fifth of the population had immigrated to Montreal within the previous six years. So much change over such a short period of time couldn't fail to leave its mark on the small town, which Montreal still was at the turn of the century.

These changes were reflected in the population's ethnic makeup. The British contingent—the English, Scots, and especially the Irish (who made up more than half of all new arrivals)—exploded. From 1831 onward, the majority of Montreal's population was British in origin and would remain so for the next 35 years.

The English-speaking population was no longer limited a handful of merchants and administrators: they were present in every class of society, swelling the ranks of artisans, as well as labourers and servants, among whom most were Irish. Moreover, the city's new ethnic makeup followed its streets and lanes: the English and Scots dominated the west, the Irish the southwest, and the French-speaking *Canadiens* the east. Needless to say, there was also some overlap between these divisions, with some French Canadians in the west and some English in the east.

The arrival of the British, quickly and en masse, also had a significant impact on Montreal's culture. The English language was everywhere. Protestant churches, schools, and associations multiplied. The city's architecture was transformed as it began to draw on British inspiration.

This turnaround led to political and ethnic tensions that climaxed in the 1830s when the Parti patriote, formerly the Parti canadien led by Louis-Joseph Papineau, headed a political struggle that culminated in the rebellions of 1837 and 1838. Essentially, the political goals of the *Patriotes*, like those of the Reformers in Upper Canada led by William Lyon Mackenzie, involved obtaining self-government for the colonies. Violence grew and the city streets became a battleground for loyalists pitted against *Patriotes*. However, the rebellions did not break out in Montreal itself—there were too many British about and the garrison was too strong—but in the surrounding area where *Canadiens* dominated. The rebellions were crushed by the military, consecrating the political victory of English-speaking Montrealers. Montreal now belonged to them.

The twin forces of immigration and economic change remoulded the city's social structure. The ranks of the business elite swelled considerably. A smattering of beaver barons gave way to a throng of merchants, some of whom were beginning to specialize. A clearer hierarchy was forming between the leading businessmen—the McGills, Molsons, Torrances, Moffatts, and Ferriers—who had a stranglehold on trade, transportation, and finance, and local merchants whose influence was more modest. The Scots and the English dominated the first group, where only a handful of *Canadiens*—Masson and Cuvillier among them—were making a name for themselves. The sphere of activity of French-Canadian merchants tended to be limited to the city itself and the immediate surrounding area.

Artisans also exploded in number thanks to the new possibilities afforded by rapid expansion. Growth was particularly pronounced in the leather and garment sectors, not to mention the metals, transportation equipment, wood, and food sectors. Construction grew in importance, employing one worker in ten. The French-speaking population dominated construction, whereas the English gained influence in the other sectors.

In what was still a pre-industrial city, the number of labourers and servants—40 percent of the workforce in 1825— was considerable. Their ranks were of course inflated by the influx of poor, unskilled Irish immigrants. Labourers found employment in transportation and construction, while servants were for the most part women and girls, mainly immigrants. Manufacturers, who multiplied throughout the 1840s, could thus count on masses of workers who formed the basis of Montreal's industrial proletariat.

Immigration also made for religious diversity. A number of Protestant churches were now active in Montreal, each with its own place of worship and organizations. Church towers sprang up across the city, most of them Protestant. The small Jewish community had its own synagogue, the first one in

IRISH MONTREAL

This engraving illustrates the 1873 spring flood in Griffintown, the main
Irish neighbourhood in Montreal. The artist reproduced the regular
stereotypes of poverty and drunkenness then associated with the Irish
people. Large numbers of Irish immigrants arrived in Montreal between
the 1820s and the 1850s and by mid-century they accounted for more than
half of the English-speaking population.

(Musée McCord, M985.230.5356)

Canada, built in 1777. But the *Canadiens* and the Irish ensured the bulk of the population remained Catholic. The Catholic Church adapted to the Irish by recruiting English-speaking priests and nuns and creating an Irish parish—Saint Patrick's—whose church was built in 1847.

The Catholic Church also had to adapt to the expanding Montreal area. Its goal was to create a separate diocese from the diocese of Quebec. First, Jean-Jacques Lartigue was named auxiliary bishop for Montreal in 1820. His nomination saw sparks fly with the Saint-Sulpice seminary, which had until then dominated religious life in Montreal. The difficulties smoothed themselves out in 1835 and Montreal finally got a bishopric of its own in 1836, although Bishop Lartigue died in 1840. His successor, Ignace Bourget, would more than leave his mark on the course of Montreal history in the decades that followed. The appointment of a bishop to Montreal led to the Saint-Jacques Cathedral being built. It opened its doors in 1825, while the Sulpicians had the new Notre Dame parish church built between 1824 and 1829 to meet growing numbers of the faithful.

A new shape

In 1792, the government redefined the boundaries of Montreal, setting them at a distance from the walls of 100 chains, based on the old British measurement, or approximately two kilometres. The new territory, an enormous rectangle, contained the old town, the suburbs, and a sizable rural area around them. This ensured Montreal had plenty of room to grow for decades to come.

The trend continued: the suburbs especially grew and in 1825 contained a little over three quarters of the population. The biggest were the suburbs of Saint-Laurent, Québec, and

Saint-Joseph. In 1831, the government divided the area into wards for the first time, and then redivided it in 1840 and, in particular, in 1845. As of 1845, Montreal had nine wards: three in the old town (West, Centre, and East) and six elsewhere (Sainte-Anne, Saint-Antoine, Saint-Laurent, Saint-Louis, Saint-Jacques, and Sainte-Marie). The town would remain divided in this way, with only minor modifications, until the end of the century.

The private sector continued to drive urban development. One notable exception was the demolition between 1801 and 1817 of the fortifications, which had become awkward and cumbersome. The government put three commissioners in charge of the project and they came up with a plan to add appeal to the areas reclaimed. Their actions would leave their mark on the city for a long time to come: canals were made out of the rivers and de la Commune, Saint-Jacques, and McGill streets were all developed, not to mention Dalhousie and Victoria squares and Champ-de-Mars.

It was also at the start of the nineteenth century that a new market was created, a market that would become Place Jacques-Cartier. The old market was reclaimed in the 1830s to build Montreal's first Customs House. In 1833, Sainte-Anne market went up at Place D'Youville. It would be home to the Parliament of Canada from 1844 to 1849, when it was torched by protesters rioting against the adoption of the Rebellion Losses Bill, devised to compensate victims of repression during the rebellions of 1837–1838. A similar bill compensating victims in Upper Canada had passed with little opposition, but when the Governor had just sanctioned the equivalent bill for Lower Canada, English Tory protesters, egged on by *The Montreal Gazette*, marched on the Parliament, broke in, and set fire to the building that also housed the library and archives. This event brought an end to Montreal's brief stint

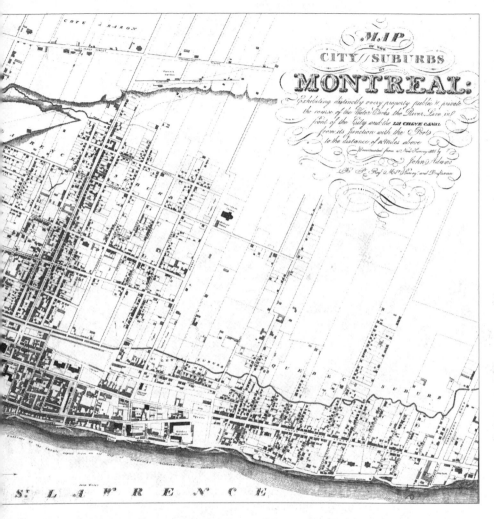

MONTREAL IN 1825

Drawn by John Adams, this map illustrates the tremendous urban expansion since the British Conquest. The walls have disappeared but the old town's shape and density are still visible. In 1825, most of the population lived in the sprawling suburbs, now within the city limits. In the lower left corner is the Lachine Canal, opened in 1825.

(Archives de la Ville de Montréal, VM66-S3P031)

PARLIAMENT BURNING, 1849

The Parliament of Canada was located in the Sainte-Anne market building (on today's Place D'Youville, in Old Montreal). Tory rioters burned it on April 25, 1849. This dramatic event illustrates the tensions between French and English-speaking Montrealers during the 1830s and 1840s. Ironically, the man who started the fire, Alfred Perry, was a volunteer fireman.

(Library and Archives Canada, C-002726, *The Illustrated London News*, 19 May, 1849) as the country's capital. In 1845, the municipal government made a start on the imposing Bonsecours market building, which would act both as City Hall and a public market.

These are only a few of the transformations to affect Old Montreal in the first half of the nineteenth century. Growing trade led merchants to erect bigger buildings for their stores and warehouses, particularly along Saint-Paul. Notre-Dame became the main shopping street, while Saint-Jacques was home to the headquarters of the first financial institutions (it was here that the Bank of Montreal had a new building built, from 1845 to 1848, opposite Place d'Armes). From the 1840s onward, merchants began to live elsewhere, moving away to what became the Golden Square Mile at the foot of Mount Royal and leaving the downtown area to commerce and city management.

The buildings of Old Montreal were built with grey stone dug up from quarries on the island. In the suburbs, on the other hand, almost every home was built with wood. The French style of home with a gable roof continued to predominate, and it was not until the 1840s that flat-roofed, British-inspired homes began to appear in rows. Over 50 years, Montreal garnered a reputation that it would hang on to for a long time to come: it became a city of tenants (some 70 percent of heads of household in 1825), due to an influx of poor people who could not afford to buy their own homes.

Managing the city

In the early nineteenth century, justices of the peace chosen by the colonial authority were still responsible for local administration. In order to take care of the needs of a city the size of Montreal, they had to adopt a growing body of regulations and to oversee a larger number of local officers (road

inspectors, constables, tax collectors, etc.). The leaders of the
Patriotes, who were fighting for a more democratic political
system, wanted these justices of the peace replaced by elected
city councillors. For their part, British merchants were cam-
paigning for a Harbour Commission. Ignoring their usual
differences, both groups joined together to support both
projects. The Harbour Commission was set up in 1830 and
the act incorporating the municipality was adopted the following year, though not applied until 1833. A first municipal
council was elected and chose Jacques Viger as mayor. The
experience was short-lived, however, since the act did not
apply beyond 1836 and political unrest prevented its renewal.
The justices of the peace recovered their previous responsibilities for a few more years.

Municipal government returned in 1840. At first, the governor chose the members of the city council, but elections
were again called as of 1843. Councillors and aldermen chose
the mayor from among their ranks and it wasn't until 1852
that citizens would elect their mayor directly. Owners and
tenants had the right to vote, provided that the value of their
property or the rent they paid was above a certain amount,
and they were barred from voting if they hadn't paid their
municipal taxes. Because of these restrictions, a considerable
segment of the population was unable to voice its opinion in
elections. From the 1840s, the city council had a majority of
English-speaking councillors. They were businessmen for the
most part and ran the Corporation of the City of Montreal
like they might have run a private company. At City Hall,
under a tacit agreement the mayor was alternately French or
English, although this was not always respected.

The municipality, funded largely through property taxes,
controlled local activities (construction, markets, keeping the
peace) and looked after the roads. Public utilities were basic-

THE GREAT FIRE OF 1852

On July 9, 1852, as waterworks were partly idle for maintenance reasons, fire broke out in two distinct neighbourhoods. At the end of the day, in Saint-Louis and Sainte-Marie wards, most of the houses had disappeared. Afterwards municipal authorities forbade the construction of wood-only houses.

(Archives du Séminaire de Québec, Tiroir 212, No. 13)

ally non-existent, and this began to cause serious problems, given the rate at which Montreal was expanding. For as long as Montreal had been little more than a small town of a few thousand souls, private initiatives and groups of individuals coming together had gotten the job done, but now the city was much more heavily populated and some problems were taking on catastrophic proportions.

As with all pre-industrial cities, Montreal was regularly buffeted by some scourge or other. This was always the case with fires. The worst broke out in 1852, destroying 1,200 homes and leaving 9,000 on the street. Montreal had no more than a few companies of volunteer firefighters, and it wasn't until 1863 that the municipality organized its own fire brigade. Plenty of water was also required to put out these fires, which was easier said than done. Montrealers got their water from the St. Lawrence and public fountains. A private water system had been in place since 1819, but it covered only part of the city. The city purchased it in 1845, but only began work on a new waterworks system in 1852, completing it in 1856. With all these measures in place, never again would the city be brought to its knees by a disaster as terrible as the Great Fire of 1852.

Epidemics also tore through the city. Cholera struck in 1832, 1834, 1849, and 1854; typhus in 1847: in all, more than 8,000 Montrealers lost their lives. More generally speaking, sanitary conditions in Montreal were atrocious. Garbage lay everywhere, raw sewage lined the streets, and public hygiene meant scarcely more than isolating the sick when epidemics struck. The city was also flooded on a regular basis, which did little to help sanitary conditions.

The massive arrival of immigrants worsened these problems and increased poverty. Private charities—religious orders in particular—did their best to relieve the misery and

WOODEN SUBURBAN HOUSE

Still standing, this suburban wooden French-style home with a gable roof
was built in the 1760s, enlarged in the 1810s, and restored in 1986. It is
located on Saint-Louis street, in the former Saint-Louis suburb. Thousands
of similar houses dominated the Montreal landscape until the mid-
nineteenth century. After the Great Fire of 1852, which wiped out many
of them, the city forbade the construction of new wood-only houses. Over
time, most of the remaining ones either disappeared or were clad with
bricks. From the 1840s on, British-style homes became the norm.

(Photo: Robin Philpot)

help those afflicted by epidemics. But they lacked numbers and resources, and it was only when Catholic charities grew, at the behest of Bishop Bourget, that these various organizations were better able to cope.

Montreal, in short, had grown too quickly, and its leaders had been caught off guard. The second half of the nineteenth century nevertheless saw a range of public utilities better meet the requirements of a large city.

CHAPTER 7

An Industrial City
1850–1896

Towards the halfway mark of the nineteenth century, Montreal began a new phase in its history, a phase that would transform it into Canada's biggest industrial centre. Its population and landscape were fashioned by forces unleashed by industrialization, with the repercussions lasting for years to come.

A big city

From 1850 onward, Montreal was becoming more and more like a big city, a metropolis even. Population climbed from 58,000 in 1852 to 107,000 in 1871 and reached 267,000 by 1901, almost 325,000 if you counted the suburbs. The change of scale was appreciable, but growth like that doesn't come steadily. A spurt in the 1850s was followed by a twenty-year lull, only for the population figures to again progress in leaps and bounds at the dawn of the 1880s and at the very end of the century.

Around 1850, immigration was still high, riding a wave of new arrivals from Ireland. But the wave had broken, and for the next few decades or so Montreal welcomed proportionately many fewer immigrants than in years past. Rural migration took up the slack, with hundreds of thousands of people

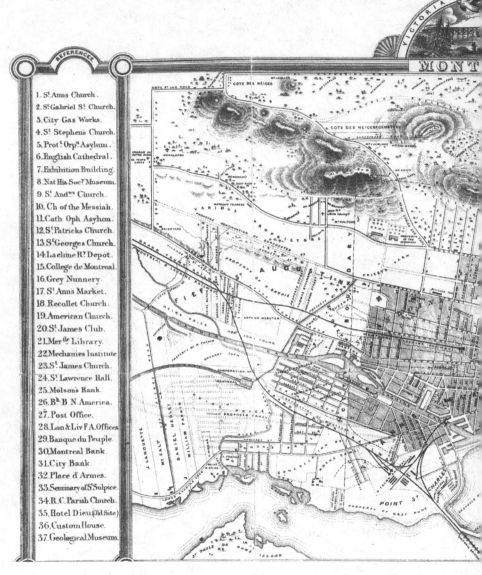

REFERENCES

1. St Anns Church.
2. St Gabriel St Church.
3. City Gas Works.
4. St Stephens Church.
5. Prot! Orph Asylum.
6. English Cathedral.
7. Exhibition Building.
8. Nat His Soc! Museum.
9. St Andws Church.
10. Ch of the Messiah.
11. Cath Oph Asylum.
12. St Patricks Church.
13. St Georges Church.
14. Lachine R! Depot.
15. College de Montreal.
16. Grey Nunnery.
17. St Anns Market.
18. Recollet Church.
19. American Church.
20. St James Club.
21. Mer de Library.
22. Mechanics Institute.
23. St James Church.
24. St Lawrence Hall.
25. Molsons Bank.
26. Bk B N America.
27. Post Office.
28. Lon & Liv FA. Offices
29. Banque du Peuple.
30. Montreal Bank.
31. City Bank.
32. Place d Armes.
33. Seminary of S Sulpice.
34. R.C. Parish Church.
35. Hotel Dieu(Old Site)
36. Custom House.
37. Geological Museum.

38. Free Church.
39. Court House.
40. Jesuits College.
41. Ladies Ben! Inst!!
42. S! Law™ Market.
43. Bon Pasteur.
44. S! James Church
45. German Church.
46. General Hospital.
47. Bonsecours Market.
48. Barracks.
49. Military Hospital.
50. S! Luke's Chapel.
51. Molson's College.
52. Molson's Church.
53. S! Johns Church.
54. Jewish Synagogue.
55. Montreal House.
56. Zion Church.
57. English Free Church.
58. Ottawa Hotel.
59. Donegana's Hotel.
60. Baptist Church.

POPULATION.

French Origin 43.070.
British and other
Origins.   47.936.
Outside Limits 10.424
TOTAL.   101.430.

1861.

Latitude 45,30, 21.N.
Longitude 72,33,30W.
Height of Mountain 750.

Published by
Starke & C? Printers
Montreal.

MONTREAL IN 1861

The city boasted some 90,000 inhabitants while 10,000 more lived in the new emerging suburbs. It still had room to grow within its limits, as urbanization was concentrated between the river and Sherbrooke street. Railways had come to town and were able to cross the St. Lawrence on the brand new Victoria Bridge, inaugurated by the Prince of Wales in 1860.

(Archives de la Ville de Montréal, BM5-3_51_C71-Inv1898-2)

leaving the countryside in the late nineteenth century in the hope of improving their lot. Most headed to the United States, but a fair few stayed in Montreal, among them English-speaking migrants from the Eastern Townships, Ontario, and the Maritimes, along with plenty of French Canadians from the rural areas surrounding Montreal.

Huge numbers of homes had to be built to accommodate these new arrivals and the children of established Montrealers, extending the city's urban sprawl. At first, they lived within the city limits but, from the 1870s on, they spilled over into new municipalities in the suburbs: Hochelaga to the east; Saint-Jean-Baptiste to the north; Saint-Gabriel, Sainte-Cunégonde, and Saint-Henri to the southwest; and others that followed. In 1891, there were already close to 70,000 people living in these new neighbourhoods. Montreal was keen to incorporate these municipalities that had sprouted up on its outskirts, annexing four of them between 1883 and 1893.

As the city's limits expanded, its homes were given a whole new look. The traditional home with a gable roof made with wood or stone had dominated for two centuries in Montreal, but was now abandoned in favour of newer designs. Flat roofs became standard, the use of brick, widespread. A new type of British-inspired terrace housing sprang up in rows in the more fashionable parts of town, with a lane running behind the lots. But the big new thing in working-class neighbourhoods was the duplex. Two-storey buildings with one apartment on top of the other spread like wildfire from the 1860s, becoming the template for many a Montreal home. The duplex spawned the triplex, each—along with variations that had up to five or six apartments—meeting the needs of a burgeoning population that almost always rented and, because of their low income, needed affordable accommodation.

This innovative architecture was not limited to housing. Commercial properties began to feature open areas, iron or steel frames, and elevators, making for bigger, taller buildings. Victorian architecture expressed itself in all its forms, especially in Old Montreal, where new warehouse stores and office buildings thrived, eliminating much of the city's French heritage along the way.

Population growth and the city's expansion as a whole required modern public utilities to meet problems that had grown in scope. A new waterworks system was inaugurated in 1856, efficiently supplying water to the whole city, and to this was added a network of underground sewers, helping to clean up living conditions. The fire department was formed in 1863, with a health board following in 1865. The municipality also managed other services, including building inspections, police, markets, and parks. Montreal's first big park, on Mount Royal, was created in 1874 and designed by the foremost American landscape architect of the day, Frederick Law Olmsted, who had also designed New York's Central Park. La Fontaine park and another on Île Sainte-Hélène soon followed.

Nevertheless, some public utilities were managed privately, which was the case for public transit. Montreal's tramways started rolling in 1861. Their cars were pulled by horses, moving across the city on rails in summer and on skates in winter. The grid spread gradually, but really started to expand after 1892, with the arrival of the faster, more efficient electric tramway. It marked the real beginning of mass transit and boosted the city's expansion by making communications easier from one end to the other. Private companies managed other services. A gas network had been up and running since 1836. Electricity, first publicly demonstrated by French-Canadian industrialist J.-A.-I. Craig in 1879, became a public utility in the 1880s and even began to replace gas for street lighting. The telephone also rang for the first time in the city in 1877.

At the end of the nineteenth century, Montreal had all the trappings of a modern city. The latest inventions, from the elevator to the electric tramway, spread across town in no time at all. And the city also had an impressive number of newspapers that published local and international news in French or English and put Montrealers in touch with the world around them.

The wheels of industry

Montreal's expansion in the second half of the nineteenth century was mainly due to the manufacturing industry setting up shop in the city. A first wave of industrialization had hit Canada in the 1840s, then a second in the 1880s. After the union of Upper Canada and Lower Canada in 1840, the domestic market reached a point where it was big enough to support local independent manufacturing in certain sectors and wean itself off imports. The market grew still further with Confederation in 1867, then again with the acquisition of the west and the integration of British Columbia. Much of this new production found a natural home in Montreal, at the heart of the country's transportation, trade, and financial networks.

These networks had been set up by Montreal businessmen and continued to grow. Montreal wholesalers, increasingly a different breed from retailers, supplied a vast number of merchants in Canada's towns, villages, and countryside. Montreal banks multiplied and opened new branches, with the Bank of Montreal remaining the biggest in the country.

Montreal's main advantage was nevertheless its strategic position as the hub of the transportation systems. Its port became the busiest in Canada, with a forest of masts bobbing on its waters each summer. The Harbour Commission improved its facilities and, in 1850 at the behest of its president, John Young, had a canal dug in the St. Lawrence River between Quebec City and Montreal. Now bigger ocean-going ships could make it as far as Montreal. Brothers Hugh and Andrew Allan set up one of the biggest transatlantic lines in Canada's history and played a very active role in many other Montreal businesses.

Not content with being a maritime hub, Montreal became a railroad hub too, the railway playing a key role in distributing manufactured goods. Canada boasted two main systems: the Grand Trunk Railway System covering southern Quebec and Ontario from 1854, and the Canadian Pacific Railway, which cut across the country and made it as far as the Vancouver area in 1886. Both had their North American head offices and main construction and maintenance workshops in Montreal, and both left their mark on the city's economy.

For its part, Montreal's manufacturing industry—with production clustered in huge, mechanized factories—really started to emerge in the 1840s. It had two main axes. The first was light industry, supported by a large labour force that was poorly paid and unskilled and largely made up of rural French Canadians. It had a number of distinct industries. Shoemaking, an old Montreal specialty if ever there was one, was the city's leading industry in 1870. The garment industry was also a major concern, scattered across a number of small workshops close to the downtown area. And the textile industry—for the most part manufacturing cotton fabrics—took hold in the suburbs where the biggest factories were, such as the Victor Hudon mill in Hochelaga. Montreal also became the biggest tobacco-processing centre in Canada, and

THE PORT IN 1884

Managed by the Harbour Commissioners, the port was a vital component
of Montreal's prosperity. It provided the main import/export link between
Canada and the United Kingdom and attracted many sea-going vessels.
Numerous *goélettes*, the local boats plying the waters between towns and
villages along the St. Lawrence River, also berthed here. The port facilities
allowed easy interconnections with the railways.

(Musée McCord, Collection Claude Bouchard, 1332)

attracted a host of industries in the vast food production sector, including flour mills, sugar refineries, breweries, distil-
leries, meatpacking, and cookie factories.

The second axis was heavy industry. It required a labour
force that was much better skilled and consequently better
paid, and workers tended to be British in origin. There were
two main sectors. The first, involving iron and steel, made
engines, railing, and pipes, along with stoves, kitchenware,
tooling, and hardware. The rolling stock sector produced
locomotives, railway cars, and parts. The diversity of industry
in Montreal was already striking, with most manufacturing
sectors represented.

All this new activity carved out an industrial landscape for
the city. Factories tended to stick close to the harbour and
railway lines, working-class homes huddling in around them.
Nowhere better illustrates the phenomenon than the area
around Lachine Canal, the birthplace of heavy industry in
Montreal. It was home to Grand Trunk Railway shops, and
other factories churning out machinery and many different
iron and steel products, not to mention spinning and knitting
mills, and the Redpath sugar refinery, while their employees
would live on the neighbouring streets. Population was just
as dense in the east end in the Sainte-Marie Ward, then in
Hochelaga, with a string of shoe and food businesses—
including the Molson brewery and the Viau cookie company—and the Canadian Pacific Angus shops. A third
industrial area developed in the north of the city, this time
dedicated to the garment industry.

A growing number of people in the labour force now
worked in factories. Working conditions were dreadful. Pay
was low, particularly for unskilled workers, of which there
was no shortage in Montreal. The wages paid to heads of
household were generally not enough for families to live

LABOUR STRIFE, 1877

Labourers working on the enlargement of the Lachine Canal went on strike
in 1877. Many of them were Irishmen. Canada was in the midst of a major
depression. Employers were trying to reduce wages and workers resisted.

(Henri Julien, Public Archives of Canada, C 7709)

decently, and so the shortfall had to be made up by sending some children and most teenagers out to work. Education levels therefore remained low. Mothers had to keep an iron grip on the family purse strings and take on sewing or laundry work at home, or take in boarders.

Workdays were long, with almost no job security to speak of. Harbour, transportation, and construction workers spent the winter unemployed, as did many factory workers. Trade unionism, a movement still in its infancy, mainly involved the skilled trades and played only a limited role in improving working conditions. In short, the average working-class family lived precariously. Disease was rampant and mortality rates, particularly among newborns, very high. Eighty percent of the population were tenants and their meagre incomes meant they could not always afford adequate housing.

In contrast, company managers and executives were living high off the hog in spacious, well-lit homes, with big gardens, servants galore, teas, banquets, and receptions. Social divides were becoming more and more pronounced in Montreal in the second half of the nineteenth century.

A British city with a French heart

In 1850, Montrealers of British origin were still in the majority. But as immigration slowed and rural migration picked up, the situation was turned on its head, with French Canadians back in the majority by 1866 and making up 60 percent of the population at century's end. In spite of this demographic change, the city still felt distinctly British in its institutions, architecture, and the predominant role played by the English language.

The might and influence of the higher echelons of the Anglo-Scots bourgeoisie were especially noticeable. The

Molsons, the Allan brothers, George Stephen, Donald Smith, and William Macdonald amassed huge fortunes by investing in a number of sectors at once. They controlled Canada-wide businesses and were very close to Britain. They and their likes lived at the foot of the mountain, in the area that would later be known as the Golden Square Mile. They frequented exclusive clubs and made generous contributions to Anglo-Protestant institutions, McGill University, and the Montreal General Hospital in particular. The Board of Trade was a much listened-to representative for this dominant class.

And yet French Canadians were keen to carve out a place for themselves in their own city. A burgeoning French-Canadian business elite played an active role in wholesale trade and certain manufacturing industries, with the likes of Rodier, Hudon, Barsalou, Rolland, and Viau being among the leading lights of French-Canadian entrepreneurship. They might not have been as powerful as their English-speaking counterparts, but they were setting up big companies operating in Montreal. New French-Canadian financial institutions backed their efforts, particularly Banque Jacques-Cartier (1861) and Banque d'Hochelaga (1874). In 1887, French-speaking businessmen also created their own board of trade, the Chambre de commerce du district de Montréal, in order to defend their interests, which the existing Board of Trade had paid little heed to.

French Canadians also began to make inroads in municipal politics. In 1882, they obtained a one-seat majority on the city council and their positions were consolidated by a series of annexations after 1883. From that moment on, nothing would ever be the same again. City councillor Raymond Préfontaine set up a solid political machine that drew support from the French-speaking masses and soon took power at City Hall. His politics were populist and aimed at seeing

French-Canadian voters and the city's east end share in the economic spinoffs generated by the major road works he had carried out.

This raised the ire of many English-speaking city councillors, who came from the world of big business. Labelling themselves reformers, they denounced the patronage practiced by Préfontaine's party and opposed expensive major public works projects. The clash between reformers and populists soon became a struggle between west and east, between the wealthy English and the French-speaking masses. These tensions would play out on the municipal stage for decades to come, but for the time being French-Canadian populists were in control.

Inter-ethnic tensions came to a head in 1885. A smallpox epidemic saw clashes, and occasional rioting, over mandatory vaccination, favoured by part of the mainly English elites and opposed by part of the French-Canadian population. That same year in November, the hanging of Metis leader Louis Riel in Regina sparked a bitter reaction among the French-Canadian population.

Generally speaking, however, both groups tended to keep largely to themselves, attending their own institutions. For French-speaking Montrealers, the Catholic Church played a key role in social life. The Catholic Church was also experiencing something of a renaissance under Bishop Bourget. The bishop bolstered the clergy's hold over life in the city, bringing several religious orders over from France and encouraging Montreal's orders to grow. After a long battle with the Sulpicians, Bourget managed to have Rome break up the parish of Notre Dame in 1865, allowing him to create more parishes and better control parishioners. He also fought long and hard for a university, and in 1876 a branch of Quebec City's Université Laval was established in Montreal. Under his episcopate, women created one new charity after another, along with social services and places of instruction of all kinds.

And so Montreal was made up of two very different worlds, with language and religion separating French-speaking Catholics from English-speaking Protestants. Each group had its own churches, its own education system all the way up to university, and its own hospitals, social services, social and cultural organizations, and newspapers. They lived apart in Montreal. Between them was the Irish community, with one foot in the English-speaking world and the other in the world of Catholicism dominated by French Canadians, but the relative size of the Irish population was waning. The small Jewish community, another group set apart by language and religion, was boosted by the arrival of a wave of immigrants from Eastern Europe in the 1880s.

Despite seemingly rigid ethnic and religious barriers, groups and individuals did interact around town—at the workplace, in stores, out on the street, and in public places—and exchanges were common. Co-existence is necessarily a dynamic process in any city. Social divides only added to the diversity, with each group having its own bourgeois and working class, its own elites high above the masses. At times, ethnic or religious solidarity overcame other barriers, while at different moments social solidarity seemed to predominate. In other words, Montreal society in the late nineteenth century was a complex whole, a juxtaposition of distinct worlds in constant interaction.

CHAPTER 8

Canada's Leading Metropolis 1896–1914

Between the end of the nineteenth century and the start of the First World War, Montreal experienced one of the strongest growth spurts in its history. Its population exploded and spread further and further from the city centre. The city was a hive of activity and reached the peak of its powers as the biggest in Canada.

Explosive growth

The numbers speak for themselves. A city that had no more than 217,000 inhabitants in 1891 (250,000 including the suburbs) had 468,000 in 1911 (528,000 with the suburbs), a gain of over a quarter of a million people in twenty years.

Needless to say, the birth rate alone couldn't explain such growth; it was tens of thousands of new arrivals that made the difference. The immigration movement in Canada had slowed considerably in the late nineteenth century, but picked up again at the start of the twentieth century to reach new heights. Part of the wave flowed into Montreal. So who exactly decided to come and live in the city? First and foremost, the English, particularly skilled workers looking for factory jobs. But Montreal also saw a new phenomenon: the arrival of

MONTREAL IN 1919

This map illustrates the extent of urbanization that occurred early in the twentieth century. A number of suburban towns experienced rapid development but many subdivisions were the result of speculation and

remained empty. The city annexed most of these towns before
1919. Among the remaining independent municipalities, many
were inhabited by a majority of English speakers.

(Archives de la Ville de Montréal, VM66-S5P144)

European immigrants not from the British Isles. Of these immigrants, by far the majority were Jews fleeing persecution in Eastern Europe, but there were also Italians, Poles, and Russians, all looking to escape the misery of their countries of origin. French and English Canadians also continued to leave the countryside for the city in droves. At the turn of the century, Montreal was a magnet for those hoping to improve their lot and start afresh.

Montreal's remarkable economic growth bore out this migration. Every sector of the city's economy was given a shot in the arm. This was the case for international trade and navigation, for example. Agricultural development in Western Canada made Montreal the country's biggest port of export for grain. To keep up with demand, the Harbour Commission had to quickly modernize its facilities and build new wharves and grain elevators. That was when what we know today as Montreal's Old Port was developed, along with the eastern section of the harbour near the suburban town of Maisonneuve. Expansion of the railways also boosted Montreal's role as Canada's transportation hub.

The manufacturing industry soared like never before. Many factories expanded to cope with growing needs and new ones—like the CPR Angus Shops or the Canadian Vickers ship-yards—sprang up, more often than not in the suburbs, where land was available. Meanwhile, Canada's rapid development helped consolidate the financial sector. Montreal banks were still undeniably leaders in the field, despite the growth of their rivals in Toronto. As the country's biggest businesses merged, spawning companies like Dominion Textile and Montreal Light, Heat, and Power, the Montreal Stock Exchange and the city's financial stakeholders grew in importance.

Montreal fully performed its role as Canada's leading metropolis. The city's financial institutions, railway companies, and wholesalers played an active role in the development of Western Canada, where branches sprung up and new markets were made available for Montreal's industrial plants. They were also involved in developing natural resources and expanding the manufacturing sector in Quebec and Ontario.

All this activity brought major changes to the city and surrounding area. The downtown was dotted with office towers where large companies had their headquarters. Rue Saint-Jacques, or St. James Street as it was then known, became Canada's business power centre, with each bank having its own distinctive building there, decorated with huge columns that aimed to show the world just how sound they were.

The industrial development along the Lachine Canal spread westward, while similar development in Sainte-Marie-Hochelaga expanded eastward towards Maisonneuve and Longue-Pointe, and the garment industry underwent a northward expansion along Saint-Laurent boulevard, also known as The Main.

The biggest phenomenon of all, though, was the extraordinary growth of the suburbs as the city underwent a population boom. Urban sprawl extended well beyond the city limits and a number of small municipalities expanded rapidly, Saint-Henri, Saint-Louis, and Maisonneuve, the biggest among them. This development came on the cusp of a new technology: the electric tramway, introduced in 1892. Streetcar lines shot out in all directions, helping people get from A to B and allowing Montrealers to live further away from their work. Montreal tried to make the most of this expansion. The annexation movement, which started between 1883 and 1893, picked up again with a vengeance in 1905 and kept going until 1918. Montreal added on 33 new areas in all, swallowing up 23 distinct municipalities in the process. When the dust settled, the city was five times bigger than in 1867.

A changing society

Population growth brought about major social change. This was particularly true about ethnic makeup, the result of migratory movement. Migration to the city from the Quebec countryside kept French Canadians at a little over 60 percent of the population. Montrealers of British stock, on the other hand, saw their share fall, even though their numbers were still growing in absolute terms: in 1901, they still made up one third of the city's population, but had dropped back to a quarter by 1911.

The sea change was brought about by the rise in other ethnic groups. Representing less than 2.5 percent of Montreal's population in the nineteenth century, they reached 5 percent in 1901 and close to 11 percent in 1911. More than half were Jews. Concentrated along Saint-Laurent boulevard, the Jewish population—Yiddish in language and culture—were mainly workers in the garment industry who lived close to their shops. They had many synagogues, cultural organizations, and charities, and even a daily Yiddish newspaper, reproducing the organizations of their Lithuanian *shtetl* in Montreal. The Italians were the other group of significance. Mainly employed in the construction industry, they started to form a neighbourhood of their own in the north end of the city and already had two parishes by 1910. Add into the mix a few thousand other Europeans and a couple of hundred Chinese, who were beginning to bunch together on La Gauchetière, and Montreal was looking more and more like a patchwork of various ethnic origins, even though groups of French and British origin continued to predominate.

Social differences remained stark. The higher echelons of the British bourgeoisie retained their dominant position. Having become much richer with the prosperity of the day, its members enjoyed luxurious lifestyles in their huge homes in the Golden Square Mile and Westmount. Individuals such as Cornelius Van Horne, Thomas Shaughnessy, Richard B. Angus, Vincent Meredith, and Herbert Holt were at the very top of Canada's social ladder, and their decisions shaped the development of the whole country.

For its part, the French-speaking bourgeoisie continued the ascent it had begun the previous century. Economic growth also gave it the opportunity to grow richer and enjoy a better lifestyle. Even though some members like Louis-Joseph Forget and Frédéric-Liguori Béique reached the heights of Canada's financial world, most owned medium-sized businesses that essentially focused on the Montreal or Quebec markets. Businessmen such as Oscar Dufresne, Hormisdas Laporte, Trefflé Berthiaume, and G.-N. Ducharme played a major role in the economics and politics of Montreal and its suburbs. Meanwhile, small neighbourhood businesses multiplied as the city expanded both in size and population.

The working class, however, continued to make up the bulk of the population. The manufacturing, transportation, and construction sectors employed the lion's share of the labour force. Skilled workers also took advantage of the favourable labour market. More and more joined trade unions, almost all of which were affiliated with international unions that had originated in the United States and were now expanding. Skilled workers took a greater interest in politics, thanks to the Labour Party and its workers' clubs. This led to Alphonse Verville, a plumber and president of the Trades and Labour Congress of Canada, being elected to the House of Commons in 1906, and to the election of carpenter Joseph Ainey, a union organizer, as a member of the city's Board of Control in 1910. For their part, labourers and unskilled factory workers had more precarious conditions, characterized by low wages, seasonal unemployment, and job insecurity. A group of white-collar office workers and store clerks was also emerging and tended to have steadier employment, but wouldn't really take off as a social group until after the First World War.

In the French-Canadian milieu and among the Irish and the Italians, the Catholic Church remained a social force. Parishes proliferated as the city grew in size and number. Religious orders also increased their numbers and endeavoured to meet the growing demand for social services and education. The Church tried to meet the challenges posed by an urban society that had become more complex and diversified, and where people were becoming more materialistic.

Archbishop Paul Bruchési tried his best to stand up to these new values, impose stricter morals, and censor newspapers and entertainment, but his efforts were not exactly a success. If the Church were to continue to control society, it would have to rely on new organizations, like the École sociale populaire (an organization dedicated to spreading the Catholic social doctrine) that sought to reconcile religion with life in the city.

City life

The social differences that characterized the population of Montreal were naturally reflected in living conditions. The grand bourgeois residence on Sherbrooke and the tiny apartment in Griffintown or in the "faubourg à m'lasse" (literally the molasses suburb) were worlds apart. The distance between them was driven home by their physical appearance. On the one hand, roomy houses boasted handsome stone facades and were surrounded by trees and lawns. On the other, poorly lit brick rowhouses were starved of greenery and had muddy lanes and yards cluttered with old wooden sheds.

But the contrast wasn't entirely black and white. Housing in Montreal covered a broad spectrum. Generally speaking, even working-class homes were improving. There was none of the overcrowding that was found in some European and American cities. Backhouses, still common in the 1890s, disappeared almost entirely. New homes, which were plentiful, better met the demands of modern living: inside toilets, baths, gas cooking, coal heating, electric lighting. These changes came gradually, though: there were still plenty of filthy, dilapidated homes to be regularly denounced by the apostles of social reform.

In fact, one of the most significant phenomena of this period was the elites becoming aware of the social problems caused by urbanization and industrialization. For years, they had been content to give to the poor, but now the voices calling for far-reaching reforms were growing louder. They gave rise to a current of social reform that set up a great many organizations and set about tackling many of the problems at the same time. Most energy was devoted to the health system, which was also the scene of the greatest advances.

It must be said that Montreal in the late nineteenth century remained a danger to public health. The mortality rate, particularly for infants, was high and more than one child in four died before turning one year old. The situation was worse for French Canadians than for other groups. In the early twentieth century, doctors stepped up their public health campaign, backed by businessmen and women associated with the feminist movements and charities. Their most distinguished spokesperson was Dr. Emmanuel-Persillier Lachapelle, founder of the Notre-Dame hospital and president of the Quebec Provincial Board of Health.

Efforts at improving hygiene concentrated on water since poor quality water was a vector for disease. Simply adding

WORKING-CLASS HOUSING

This photograph was taken in 1930 in the working-class neighborhood of Hochelaga, in the east end of the city. It shows typical late nineteenth or early twentieth-century Montreal houses. Three storeys high, they usually have three to five dwellings, most of these rented out. Some are adorned with elegant woodworking.

(Archives de la Ville de Montréal, VM98-Y_2P034)

chlorine to the city's water in 1910 was enough to reduce the mortality rate. A few years later, filtration further improved the quality of the water available in Montreal and its suburbs. To improve the health of the city's children, two specialized hospitals were set up at the start of the century and in 1910 a network of free community clinics—*Les Gouttes de lait* (literally, "the drops of milk")—was tasked with handing out pasteurized milk and making families more aware of good hygiene. Information campaigns came thick and fast, aimed at mothers in particular. The public hygiene movement led the city to take on more employees and scale up inspection and prevention activities at its public health unit. On the eve of the First World War, public health still had a long way to go, but the city had begun to put things right and the fruits of the campaign would be there for all to see in years to come.

Social inequality was also visible in the world of education, with pronounced differences between Protestant and Catholic schools. Since each school board was funded largely by a property tax collected from members of their religious denomination, Protestant schools had much greater resources, which had an influence on the quality of equipment at their disposal and on teachers' salaries. The underfunded Catholic school commission paid poorly and its schools were overcrowded. Moreover, the rise in the number of pupils worsened the situation. Here, too, reformers tried to step in to improve the quality of teaching programs, teacher training, and school management, but they came up against stiff resistance from the Church, which saw education as a matter for it and it alone. In spite of everything, reforms were introduced, although their effects would mostly be felt after 1914.

The reform movement also questioned the treatment of women as second-class citizens. At the start of the twentieth century, Montreal was a hotbed of Canadian feminism. The

Montreal Local Council of Women, founded in 1893 and aimed at the English for the most part, was joined by the Fédération nationale Saint-Jean-Baptiste, created in 1907 to reach out to the French-speaking population. Both organizations battled to have women's political and legal rights recognized, and to allow them access to higher education and professional occupations. They played a very active role in the social reform movements. Key Montreal feminists were Marie Gérin-Lajoie and Julia Drummond, although countless other women, most of whom were comfortably well off, played their part too.

Along with these changes to the social landscape, the cultural world was burgeoning. A real French-language popular culture was emerging, one that was unique to Montreal. Resolutely urban, this culture still drew on French-Canadian traditions, but looked increasingly to the United States for inspiration. Mass-market newspapers played a key role in this cultural affirmation. Popular newspapers, especially *La Presse* and *La Patrie* in French and *The Montreal Star* in English, reached most homes and put forward a modernist vision of society. They were also devoting more and more space to a phenomenon that would become a major part of any city's culture: professional sports. Long the preserve of well-heeled (usually English) amateur athletes and fans, sport was now well organized, with teams, stadiums, stars, and fans. Hockey was growing in popularity, to the detriment of lacrosse, and on its way to becoming Canada's national sport.

Cinema was another novelty that carved a place for itself in Montreal in 1906 with the opening of the Ouimetoscope. Movies were hugely popular and theatres appeared all over the city to cope with the demands of a people in search of entertainment. Movies were only a part of the commercialization of leisure activities, another side of which was shown

with the opening of amusement parks like Dominion Park in
1906.

The development of municipal parks encouraged leisure
activities. Many other parks came to join the ranks of the
biggest—Mont-Royal, La Fontaine, and Île Sainte-Hélène—
and the city opened its first playgrounds.

The start of the century was also a vibrant time for upper-
class culture. The theatre was going through something of a
golden age, with one professional theatre company being set
up after the next. Literary life also enjoyed a boom thanks to
the meetings of the École littéraire de Montréal, which
included many literary figures such as Émile Nelligan.
Montrealers were also able to enjoy their own new symphony
orchestra and opera company. On the whole, however, cultural productions in Montreal remained limited and the
public mainly relied on touring foreign productions and lit-
erature from France, Britain, and the United States.

A lively political scene

The social and ethnic divisions that characterized Montreal
were naturally reflected in political life as the struggle between
populists and reformers continued and even intensified.
Montreal's most popular politician, Raymond Préfontaine,
became mayor in 1898 and held the position until 1902 when
he retired from municipal life. The political machine he had
built fell apart, however, with electoral victories for the
reformers in 1898 and 1900. The reformers managed to bring
on board a number of French-Canadian businessmen, led by
Hormidas Laporte, an alderman from 1897 and mayor from
1904 to 1906. Laporte and his colleague Herbert Brown Ames,
leader of the English-speaking reformers, tried to clean up
the city's finances and improve the services it provided,

particularly when it came to public health. They also took on the big businesses running the public utilities: gas, electricity, the tramway, and water (in the annexed districts). Many citizens, backed by certain newspapers, accused these businesses of not offering services in line with the needs of a rapidly growing population and of overcharging to obtain enormous profits. But these powerful companies belonging to Montreal's leading financiers held a monopoly and were able to hold off the critics and maintain strong support among city councillors, giving in to only a few concessions.

By 1904, the reform movement ran out of steam. New populist politicians, close to their voters and deeply rooted in their wards, appeared on the city council. The annexation of a number of towns in the suburbs brought with it more city councillors and made managing Montreal a more complex affair. Patronage again flourished at City Hall, sparking the rebirth of the reform movement under the auspices of both the English Board of Trade and the French Chambre de commerce.

In 1909, the reformers succeeded in having a public inquiry into Montreal's administration set up. Judge L. J. Cannon presided the inquiry. His report shed light on a regime of corruption and favouritism and pointed the finger at a number of city councillors. The inquiry opened the ears of many Montrealers to the reformers' arguments.

The reformers wanted to reorganize the municipal government. They sought to limit the influence of local politicians by reducing the number of seats reserved for them on the city council and by transferring some of their powers to a Board of Control elected by the people. In doing so, they hoped to eliminate waste and ensure the city was run like a business. This major reform was approved by referendum and came into effect in 1910.

In the 1910 elections, on the back of the Cannon inquiry that had discredited the current set of politicians, the reformers saw four of their candidates elected as controllers and made gains in practically every ward of the city. The "rule of honest folks" was underway, and would last until 1914. The new administration helped to improve management of the city and to reorganize the civil service. But it struggled to live up to the population's expectations for roads and public amenities. By becoming more bureaucratic, it lost sight of the needs of voters, which explains the recovery in the popularity of traditional politicians from 1914.

Between 1896 and 1914, Montreal grew rapidly, in terms of demography, its economy, and the area it covered. With half a million people, Montreal society was becoming increasingly diverse, more complex, and harder to govern. Inequalities were still there for all to see, but the efforts of reform groups were starting to bear fruit and living conditions were improving. Montreal was therefore a dynamic, lively city. It was at a crossroads not only for French and British traditions, but also for the influences of American culture and the contributions of new immigrants.

TRAFFIC JAM IN 1925

On Notre-Dame street, near Place d'Armes, automobile drivers tried to find a way around tramways (also known as streetcars) and parked cars. They were a minority at the time, but in the long run they would claim victory. Tramways, perceived as an impediment to smooth traffic, would disappear from Montreal streets by 1959.

(Archives de la Ville de Montréal, VM94-Z464)

CHAPTER 9

A North American City
1914–1929

The First World War curbed the sustained period of growth Montreal had enjoyed since the end of the nineteenth century. The city then went through a difficult spell that lasted until the start of the 1920s, which saw Montreal continue its expansion. It now had one million inhabitants and looked every bit a major North American city.

World War I

The economic slowdown was felt starting in 1913, as property values—swollen by rampant speculation—crumbled. Unemployment increased and things continued like this until at least 1915. The outbreak of war in 1914 only worsened the situation. New investments plunged, all the more so because Great Britain, which had largely funded Canada's expansion at the turn of the century, stopped exporting capital in order to devote its full attention to the war effort. Commercial and industrial activity was dented by the slowdown.

Construction stalled, bringing a temporary halt to urban expansion. Maisonneuve, a large town in Montreal's east-end suburbs that had invested heavily in the hopes of sustained growth, collapsed under its debt and even had to borrow to pay the interest on it, which led to the municipality being swallowed up by Montreal in 1918. The war also halted immigration, which had until then helped swell population numbers. Some recent immigrants were even called up and had to return to their countries of origin.

Starting in 1915, the economy picked up again. Manufacturing companies lapped up lucrative war contracts; longshoremen dispatched farm commodities and military materiel to Britain; thousands of men who signed up left their jobs to others, including a growing number of women, bringing down unemployment. War did drive up inflation, however, which had an impact on many Montreal workers whose wages were no longer enough to make ends meet.

Most of the consequences of war were political, though. Montreal was split into two camps, with the English on one side, eager for Canada to be involved to the hilt, and the French Canadians, opposed to the war, on the other. Since the turn of the century the imperialist movement had gained strength in English Canada. Anglo-Montrealers had thus felt their attachment to the British Empire grow and enlisted eagerly to fight for their homeland. Leading businessmen headed patriotic organizations and raised substantial sums to support the war effort. But Anglo-Montrealers paid a heavy price for their zeal. The war proved to be a bloodbath, with a great many young Montrealers leaving their lives on the battlefields or returning home broken by war gases and injury.

Meanwhile, despite support for the war effort from some of their leaders and intense propaganda encouraging them to enlist, French Canadians were reluctant to become involved. For them, the war was a British matter, of no concern to them. For more than 15 years, the leading lights of the nationalist movement, headed by Henri Bourassa, had been telling them that Canada should not be getting involved in wars led by the British Empire. The Canadian army, whose working language was English, was also an unappealing destination for many. The fate that awaited French-Canadian minorities from Ontario and the other provinces, whose language rights were denied, further poisoned relations between the two sides. (Nationalists even coined the term "Prussians of Ontario" to describe the people responsible for that province's language policy.)

The atmosphere soon soured. The English-language press openly attacked French Canadians who, in its eyes, were not doing their share. In fact, many French Canadians enlisted, but in much smaller proportions than English Canadians. The decision of the federal government in 1917 to impose conscription for overseas service sent sparks flying among French Canadians, massively opposed to the measure. Huge anti-conscription demonstrations were held in the city. A small group led by Élie Lalumière even resorted to terrorism, but was quickly dismantled. Ethnic tensions had reached an all-time high.

The dichotomy between English and French had been part of life in Montreal for a long time. In 1914, populist Médéric Martin exploited it adroitly when he threw his hat in the ring for mayor. He ran as the candidate of working-class French Canadians up against the rich English businessmen, defending the interests of east-end Montreal against those of the west. The French-Canadian masses swept him to a resounding victory. His election was symbolic since it brought to an end the practice of alternating between an English-speaking and a French-speaking mayor. From 1914 until the arrival of Michael Appelbaum in 2012, all future mayors would come from a French-Canadian background.

Painful adjustments

The end of the war in 1918 marked the start of a series of painful adjustments. The shift to a peacetime economy was not without its downsides, and manufacturing stalled. Soldiers returning home upset the job market. Inflation, which had reached worrying levels during the conflict (18 percent in 1917), continued to take its toll. And such a context inevitably heightened social tensions, which came to a head in 1919. That year, a record number of strikes hit Montreal, a year writ large in the annals of unions across the country because of the famous Winnipeg General Strike.

This period of adjustment resulted in a serious economic crisis from 1920 to 1922. Inflation was stopped in its tracks and prices tumbled, while unemployment skyrocketed. Private organizations struggled to help the destitute, leading the Quebec government to pass the Public Charges Act of 1921.

Economic difficulties particularly affected one of the mainstays of the Canadian economy: the railways, which had been a driver of investment before the war. Between 1917 and 1922, the federal government had to bring the Canadian Northern Railway and the Grand Trunk Railway System under government control, then integrate them into the Canadian National Railways. Happily for Montreal, the city was home to the company's new headquarters and kept its role as the railway centre, since the two main networks, Canadian Pacific and Canadian National, were headquartered there.

Postwar tensions also played out in municipal politics. Médéric Martin's election as mayor cemented the failure of the reformers, who had taken power in 1910. But the business community wasn't lying down just yet and called on the government to intervene and reform the city's administration. Montreal's rapid expansion at the turn of the century and its many annexations, particularly the annexation of Maisonneuve in 1918, had burdened the city with a heavy financial load that had the banks worried.

In 1918, the Quebec government reacted to this pressure by putting Montreal in trusteeship. The Board of Control was abolished and replaced by a five-member administrative commission, all appointed by the government. The commission had the first and last word on managing the city, and municipal elected officials saw their powers dwindle. Montreal politicians reacted vehemently to this attack on municipal autonomy that had taken the control over patronage out of their hands. Unaccountable to voters, the commissioners went about cleaning up the city's finances and reforming its administration. They quickly grew unpopular, forcing the government to terminate their mandate in 1921.

Renewed growth

Once the crisis of 1920–1922 was over, Montreal was back on the path to growth. Between 1921 and 1931, the city's population increased from 619,000 to 819,000, with the population on the whole island reaching one million people by the end of the decade.

External forces were clearly at work. As before the war, many migrated from the Quebec countryside to the city lights, and lots of English-speaking people came from other provinces to settle in the growing metropolis. Montreal reaped the rewards of a new wave of immigration that, although weaker than the one at the start of the century, was similar in makeup if not in scope, with most new arrivals hailing from Britain and eastern and southern Europe.

This increase in population naturally relaunched urban development. Urbanization mainly took place within the city

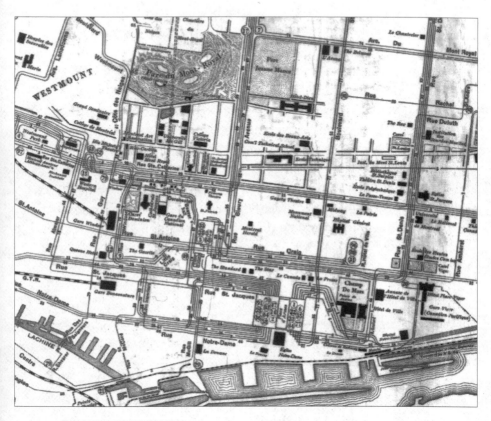

TRAMWAY LINES IN 1923

This map shows that a large number of streetcar lines were converging downtown at Place d'Armes, in Old Montreal, where the major office buildings were located. Many lines were also running on major thoroughfares, such as Saint-Denis and Sainte-Catherine streets along which the subway (Métro) system would be built in the 1960s.

limits since Montreal had annexed most of the municipalities in its suburbs and thus had vast areas of land to develop. The districts of Notre-Dame-de-Grâce and Villeray in particular were bespeckled with thousands of new homes. The tramway network whisked workers between their homes and work, and housewives to commercial thoroughfares like Sainte-Catherine, the mecca of Montreal shopping. In addition each neighbourhood had its nexus of local retail stores and services located on a busy street, such as Notre-Dame in Saint-Henri, Mont-Royal on the Plateau, and Ontario in Sainte-Marie.

Revival of the construction industry affected more than just the residential sector. Schools and hospitals went up, along with a host of commercial and industrial buildings. The downtown area continued its makeover with the erection of shiny new skyscrapers, built in the American style, that transformed the skyline. The Victorian era had well and truly ended and Montreal was looking more and more like a bustling North American city by the day. The downtown area now spilled over from Old Montreal toward uptown Sainte-Catherine street, between Phillips and Dominion squares, with department stores squeezed in between the office towers.

Downtown was a testament to the city's economic—and, above all—financial strength. Montreal was still Canada's largest city, although it was increasingly having to share this title with Toronto. Most major American investment in Canada ended up in Toronto, particularly in the automobile and mining industries, allowing that city to eat into Montreal's lead.

Increased financial concentration marked the 1920s. Companies such as the Bank of Montreal, the Royal Bank, Sun Life, and Bell Telephone were becoming gigantesque. Concentration also affected a string of manufacturing and

SAINTE-CATHERINE STREET IN 1930

Since late nineteenth century, Sainte-Catherine had become Montreal's unrivalled retail street. By 1930 it was lined with large department stores—such as Morgan's, Eaton's, Simpson's, Ogilvy's—and office buildings whose ground floors housed smaller independent stores. Here at the corner of Stanley, the street was lively despite the depression, which was beginning to strike the city.

(Archives de la Ville de Montréal, VM94-Z1820)

commercial businesses. Given this, French-Canadian entrepreneurs were largely peripheral figures, confined mostly to small and medium businesses.

Big businesses had more and more managers working out of downtown offices. This meant that the 1920s saw the emergence of a new social group: white-collar workers, whose numbers rose to new heights. Thousands of clerks, secretaries, telephone operators, and bookkeepers completely transformed a Montreal working environment that had until then been characterized by its sizable working class. Other services—stores of all kinds, transportation, teaching, personal services—also employed more and more people.

The decade was also marked by the rapid development of the middle class—which included not only professionals and local storekeepers, but a growing number of self-employed workers such as insurance agents—and executives from the public and private sectors. All shared in the city's renewed prosperity.

A better life

Living conditions showed a marked improvement. Of course, many Montrealers still had to make do with modest wages and cope with seasonal unemployment. As consumers, they were limited and scraped by on the bare necessities. Despite these difficulties, the prosperity was a boon to them, improving job security and living conditions as a whole.

The clearest sign of this improvement was the decline in mortality rates, particularly among infants, the result of public health measures implemented at the start of the century. Montreal was still burdened with a higher mortality rate than in other North American cities. Yet the progress since the late nineteenth century was striking: whereas fewer than 75 percent of children lived to be more than a year old in the 1890s, 86 percent reached their first birthday by the late 1920s. Despite a fall in infectious diseases, tuberculosis continued to rage, striking the poorest neighbourhoods hardest.

Housing also continued to improve. By the end of the decade, almost all homes had electricity, compared to only a quarter in 1914. The construction of thousands of modern buildings in the 1920s further raised standards.

Education also made leaps and bounds, even though French-speaking Catholics still lagged behind Anglo-Protestants. More and more children made it through the sixth grade and the Montreal Catholic School Commission developed secondary schools, although only a minority of students attended. Vocational education rose in popularity, and new classical colleges opened their doors.

Changes in higher education came too, with the founding of the Université de Montréal in 1920, which at last became independent from Université Laval. This change in status made it easier for the university to gather donations and to start work on a new building designed by the architect Ernest Cormier and located on the northwest flank of Mount Royal. It was also able to set up new faculties. Within a few years, the Université de Montréal had become the centre of French-Canadian intellectual life in the city and was at the heart of the scientific awakening around Brother Marie-Victorin, who later founded Montreal's Botanical Garden. Professors such as Lionel Groulx and Édouard Montpetit became household names.

The intellectual boom among French Canadians in the 1920s was still largely stoked by France, but American culture was increasingly making its presence felt in working-class circles. Although not new, the phenomenon was growing. Burlesque shows, one of the most popular forms of entertainment, were American in origin and adapted into French by

Montreal artists. Cinema, which was also growing in popularity, was dominated by American distributors who showed American movies for the most part. Radio was an emerging medium that featured programs from the United States, prompting Montrealers to rush and learn the Charleston. Generally speaking, the influence of the United States affected Montrealers' way of life. Ford and General Motors automobiles, Chiclets chewing gum, Coca-Cola, and many other American products—some of which were made in Canadian branch plants—became symbols of a modern age.

Meanwhile, British influence remained strong on the English-language cultural scene, particularly at McGill University, but American influences were increasingly making themselves felt there too, while a handful of intellectuals tried to speak up for a voice specific to Canada. Eastern European Jews, who made up the biggest group that was neither of French or British origin, also had a cultural scene all its own, drawing heavily on the Yiddish language and on Jewish and European traditions since so many immigrants were new arrivals.

In terms of social and cultural values, Montreal was therefore a lively place to be in the twenties. An important phenomenon was the delicate transformation of French-Canadian society in Montreal, which enjoyed better living standards and had a culture all its own, a culture that was more urban and North American than anywhere else in Quebec. French Canadians were looking to assert themselves in the face of the domination exerted by English Canadians. A new nationalism, more Québécois than at the start of the century, took root in Montreal around leading thinker Lionel Groulx, a priest and historian. For its part, the Société Saint-Jean-Baptiste sought to spur on national pride by reviving the tradition of Saint-Jean parades and erecting a cross on Mount Royal (1924).

French Canadians dominated municipal politics by then. Montreal regained its autonomy in 1921, when the administrative commission was abolished and elected officials again took up the reins of power. The city was now managed by an executive committee whose members were chosen by and from among the city councillors. The mayor's role was now largely symbolic, but a great deal of prestige still came with the title. Médéric Martin was mayor from 1914. Though defeated in the 1924 elections, he returned to power two years later. Then in 1928, Camillien Houde, another populist politician, defeated him. With his powerful personality, Camillien Houde would leave his imprint on the city for the next two decades.

And so the 1920s gave Montrealers a glimpse of a better life to come, for French Canadians in particular. The decade ended, however, with stock market speculation rampant... A rude awakening was just around the corner.

CHAPTER 10

Depression and War
1930–1945

From 1930 onwards, Montreal went through a rocky period that would last for some 15 years. The Great Depression nipped the hopes of the previous decade in the bud and plunged the city into a profound slump that affected its population to varying degrees. The seemingly endless depression was followed by the Second World War, which brought prosperity back, but only further delayed a return to normal life.

The Depression

The stock market crash of October 1929 marked the official beginning of the depression, but its seeds were sown in the excesses of the 1920s. From 1930 to 1933, the economy collapsed—and recovery would be painfully slow. Montreal was particularly affected: at the height of the depression, between one quarter and one third of its workforce was unemployed.

Given the key role the city played in selling Canada's raw materials abroad, Montreal took the full brunt of the worldwide slump that hit this sector. The industries that depended on the handling and shipping of these staple products, such as the manufacture of railway rolling stock, had ground to a standstill, while other sectors of the economy were indirectly affected to varying degrees. With the vast majority of workers living on low wages, the city was very vulnerable indeed to a prolonged bout of unemployment. With no savings, these people were quickly poverty-stricken and could not be relied upon to reboot the consumer market.

Consequently, city growth came to a standstill. The island's population (1,117,000 in 1941) increased by a mere 113,000 inhabitants over the course of the decade and the population of the city itself (903,000 in 1941) by only 85,000. Immigration more or less came to a complete halt, and some immigrants who had arrived in the 1920s went as far as returning to their countries of origin. Migration from the countryside to the city was also interrupted: farmers' sons and daughters saw no interest in moving to a city that offered nothing but misery, and many others preferred to go back to the farm where they could at least find something to eat. Those born and bred in Montreal, meanwhile, tended to put off marriages and have fewer children.

In such circumstances, the construction industry was very quiet indeed. Eight percent of the labour force worked in construction, not counting related industries such as manufacturing and retail of materials. Very few new homes went up during the depression and existing ones fell into disrepair since owners, who couldn't collect rent and often lost their properties altogether, had little interest in investing in repairs.

Living standards were declining. Many unemployed working-class families had to find cheaper places to live and buy the bare minimum of food, clothes, and furniture.

Charities like the St. Vincent de Paul and others that traditionally helped the destitute were quickly unable to cope with the levels of poverty raging in Montreal. From 1930 on, different levels of government had to get involved. First, they chose to give workers direct assistance via charities, but starting in 1933 the city itself took charge of distributing this direct help by setting up the Unemployment Commission. The city also set up public works programs—building overpasses and public buildings, landscaping parks, and the like—that were funded in part by the federal and provincial governments and that gave jobs to thousands of the unemployed. Such programs led to the development of Montreal's Botanical Garden and construction of the chalet on Mount Royal, for example, not to mention street urinals (what Parisians referred to as *vespasiennes* and Montrealers more cheekily called *camilliennes*, after Mayor Camillien Houde).

A shaken society

Insecurity and poverty therefore characterized the thirties. Those who still had a job saw their wages gouged and feared for the future, which hardly encouraged them to be consumers. French Canadians were hit harder than the English because they tended to have less money and more of them worked in construction and transportation. Factory workers were also more affected than service workers like teachers and civil servants who, even though they were not well paid, still had stable jobs. The middle class, which had ridden the wave of prosperity in the 1920s, was now crippled by the depression, especially the French Canadians. Customers of small stores and professionals had a hard time paying their bills and bought less. For many, the 1930s were synonymous with social decline and even bankruptcy.

It was a time of broken dreams. The hopes of a better life that the 1920s had spawned quickly dissipated. Many young people had to give up promising studies; couples had to postpone wedding plans. The depression reined in aspirations. The most popular singer of the 1930s, La Bolduc, then known as the Queen of Canadian Folksingers, voiced the helplessness a whole generation was feeling.

Some found hope in religion as hard times upped religious fervour. Crowds flocked to St. Joseph's Oratory, among them pilgrims needing a miracle. In 1937, the death of the oratory's founder, Brother André, deeply touched Quebec and hundreds of thousands of Montrealers came to pay homage to him one last time.

The Church was also going through a difficult time. Its charities were struggling to meet the needs of the destitute and had to make do with reduced resources as needs soared. The situation was made worse by the fact that certain religious orders and parishes had not invested wisely and were having financial troubles of their own. Members of the clergy intervened in public debates all the same and put forward solutions to the interminable crisis. For example, the École sociale populaire, headed by the Jesuit Joseph-Papin Archambault, put forward its social restoration program in 1933.

The crisis also roused a strong nationalist movement. Its leading light, priest and historian Lionel Groulx, inspired a whole generation of young nationalists like André Laurendeau and Paul Gouin, who would go on to make their mark on politics. The Jeune-Canada movement was founded in 1932 to express the frustrations of young French Canadians towards a society that appeared to have little to offer them. It channelled French Canadians' demands and spoke out at their exploitation by large monopolies controlled by English Canadians.

Economic difficulties also revived ethnic tensions across a city where linguistic divisions often papered over the cracks of social divides. The traditional rivalry between French and English Canadians reared its head in a host of ways, political nominations and how public funds were to be spent, among them. For example, the appointment of the first French

Canadian as president of the Harbour Commission provoked
the ire of the English-language press, which deemed the post
to belong by rights to an English Canadian, while the appointment of a unilingual English-speaking head manager of the
Montreal customs office was perceived by the French-
language press to be an insult to French Canadians.

Another type of intolerance also expressed itself more
openly in some people's attitude towards Jews. The thirties were
blighted by an upsurge in anti-Semitism across Western countries, and Montreal was not spared: though covert discrimination was a fact of life in English-language organizations, some
French-Canadian leaders came out with anti-Semitic state-
ments, Jewish businesses were attacked. There was, however,
none of the widespread violence that many European countries
endured. Tensions were somewhat eased by the open-minded-
ness shown by parts of the press and the public as a whole, as
well as cooperation among ethnic groups who demonstrated
side by side in the trade union movement.

Anti-Semitism was but one face of a troubled 1930s society,
however. A potent cocktail of ideas and movements, ranging
from the extreme left to the extreme right, was exploding all
over town. Although limited in number, communists were
making headway and spreading their message at assemblies
and in publications and organizing groups for the unemployed and factory workers. Socialists were also making their
voices heard and became more organized with the creation
of the CCF, the Co-operative Commonwealth Foundation, in
1933. The two groups were especially active among English
Canadian intellectuals and within the Jewish community,
already familiar with leftist ideas from its time in Europe.
And it was in the Cartier riding in a Jewish and French-
Canadian neighbourhood that Montreal's—and Canada's—
lone communist MP, Fred Rose, was elected in 1943. It was

also here among the communists of Montreal that renowned doctor Norman Bethune began the thought process that would lead him first to Spain with the Mackenzie-Papineau battalion that fought in the civil war that was raging, then to China where he died. The parties of the left had a hard time making inroads with French Canadians whose distinctive cultural identity and aspirations they didn't really grasp. Communists in particular also met with fierce resistance from the Catholic Church.

At the other end of the political spectrum were the fascists, who won over followers within parts of the Italian community, and a Nazi-inspired group led by journalist Adrien Arcand. Both were fringe groups, but managed to grab the headlines.

In French-Canadian circles, reactions to the crisis came mainly from the nationalists and the École sociale populaire, which proposed a Christian approach to social problems that drew on papal encyclicals. They both put forward a traditional vision of the French-Canadian nation, while also exploring novel solutions, leading a campaign to bring public utilities— notably electricity—under government control, for example, as was already the case in other large cities such as Toronto.

A city in trouble

The upheavals that were upsetting Montreal society also shook up the political scene. Voters at all levels expressed their discontent by switching governments. At the municipal level, the eventful career of Camillien Houde was typical of the turbulent times. Mayor of Montreal since 1928, he was defeated by Fernand Rinfret in the 1932 elections before winning back his post in 1934, only to lose it again in 1936, this time to Adhémar Raynault. But Houde never gave up and was back as mayor by 1938.

Houde upheld the tradition of populist politicians by fighting for the little guy and for French Canadians. Like other populists before him, he met with resistance from the elites, particularly the English-speaking business establishment. How the city was managed was again front and centre in the debate.

It must be said that the depression had sacked the city's finances. Montreal had to pay a fair chunk of unemployment assistance, but its revenues were not enough and it consistently had to borrow to make up the shortfall. For years, property taxes had been too low to meet the needs of a city the size of Montreal, which had been growing rapidly since the turn of the century. Religious, educational, and social organizations were exempt from property tax, yet they all enjoyed access to municipal services. Throughout the crisis, tax collection was tricky and property values plummeted as the city's debt rose.

Business circles blamed the state of affairs on politicians' mismanagement and the cost of patronage; they clamoured for expenditures to be slashed. For his part, Mayor Houde pointed the finger at the high costs of helping the unemployed. He stood up for the jobless and refused to reduce the already meagre help meted out to them. Instead, he tried to get the provincial and federal governments to increase their contributions, but in vain. And so, in 1935, he resigned himself to imposing a series of new taxes, including, for the first time in the history of Quebec, a sales tax. Nevertheless, these measures were not enough to right the municipality's finances before the decade was out.

In 1940, Montreal was unable to repay maturing debts when the banks refused to lend the city more money. For the banks, it was a means of leaning on the provincial government so that it would change the way the city was managed. Montreal was put under the trusteeship of the Municipal

THE CANADIAN WALL STREET

For more than a century, Saint-Jacques (known as St. James) street was the symbol of financial might in Canada. It attracted the highest concentration of wealth and power in the country. The street landscape is shown here circa 1930. It is dominated by the skyscraper built in 1926-1928 to house the head office of the Royal Bank of Canada that had just passed the Bank of Montreal as the largest financial institution in the country.

(Archives de la Ville de Montréal, VM94-Z1582)

Commission and would remain there until 1944. The city council was also overhauled. It now had three categories of city councillors, each with a third of the seats. Category A councillors were elected by property owners alone, Category B by both owners and tenants, and Category C by university, employers, and trade union organizations. This major reform removed power from the populists' hands and boosted the say of property owners, the business community, and English-speaking Montrealers.

World War II

In 1940, the economy was again transformed: Canada was at war. And the Second World War (1939–1945) had a bigger impact than the war of 1914–1918, both in Montreal and across Canada.

Montreal factories, still running almost on idle at the end of the 1930s, now had to work flat out to meet the growing demands of an economy entirely focused on the war effort and meeting the Allies' needs. Munitions factories were built, a brand new Canadair airplane factory went up in Saint-Laurent, and the Canadian Vickers shipyards—like Canadian Pacific's Angus Shops—churned out military materiel. In all, Montreal's heavy industry grew strongly. French geographer Raoul Blanchard has calculated that 38 percent of the manufacturing labour force in and around Montreal was either employed by the metallurgical industry or was making transportation equipment and electric appliances.

Light industry also benefited from the favourable market conditions. It produced khaki fabric along with army boots and uniforms while civilian production climbed as consumer demand increased.

The war brought with it a return in prosperity, putting an end to years of crisis. Full employment replaced high unemployment levels. Workers enjoyed stable jobs, good wages, and the possibility of overtime. Income levels for the population as a whole shot up. Even the municipality profited. Money no longer had to be spent on unemployment assistance and Montrealers were again able to pay their taxes, turning the city's finances around under the watchful eye of the Municipal Commission.

But the war again raised the issue of Canada's involvement. Even though French Canadians enlisted in greater numbers than for the previous conflict, enrolment rates were still proportionally lower than those of English Canadians, causing, as in 1914–1918, ethnic tensions. In 1940, Mayor Camillien Houde publicly came out against national registration and was arrested and sent to an internment camp, where he remained until 1944. A considerable number of Montreal Italians, suspected of sympathizing with the enemy, and communists, mostly Jewish, were also arrested and interned at that time.

Conscription for overseas service was again front and centre in the debate. Most French Canadians were against it, most English Canadians for it. In 1942, the federal government organized a plebiscite in which it asked all Canadians to release it from the promise it had made not to impose conscription. Montreal's nationalists—led by Maxime Raymond, André Laurendeau, and others—spearheaded resistance and played a key role in organizing the Ligue pour la défense du Canada. Widespread public assemblies for the "no" camp were held in Montreal. In the April 1942 vote, 72.9 percent of Quebec residents opposed conscription, while in the other provinces 80 percent voted in favour. In Montreal, only the western English-speaking districts were in favour. Conscription for overseas service would eventually be imposed in 1944, this time without the violence the city had seen in 1917.

Perhaps this time around Montrealers found it easier to accept the price of a war that was bringing them prosperity. It should also be mentioned that government propaganda was intense and probably convinced a good number of citizens of the conflict's importance. Radio was an important propaganda instrument. In the 1930s, radio had become part of the mass media and, despite the crisis, had found a home in many Montreal households (85 percent of which had one in 1941). At first a means of entertainment featuring music and very popular radio dramas, it also became a means of education. During the war, entertainment was overtaken by the news, helping make Montrealers aware of realities abroad.

An increased interest in the world around it was only one of the social changes the war brought to Montreal. Women joined the workforce more than ever, and the war industry offered them better-paid jobs than the positions they had traditionally filled. All women, housewives in particular, were also asked to contribute to the war effort in their own way, by recycling, taking in boarders, or volunteering.

Rationing was also part of life in wartime Montreal, although most Montreal workers found it easy to endure after the hardships of the depression. There was more food to go around and restrictions mainly affected durable consumer goods. With higher incomes that they could not spend in their entirety due to rationing, Montrealers set aside savings that would later boost the postwar economy.

Things took a more dramatic turn when it came to housing. Construction grinding to a halt during the depression had started to pose serious problems in the late 1930s, when there were too few homes to keep up with demand. The situation worsened during the war, with building materials needed by the military. A serious housing crisis would play a leading role in the explosion of urbanization after 1945.

WARTIME TRANSPORTATION

In 1944, on Sainte-Catherine, tramways reigned supreme. Wartime controls imposed severe restrictions on the use of private cars and more people than ever used public transit to get around. Automobiles would come back with a vengeance in the postwar period.

(Archives de la Ville de Montréal, VM94-Z1818)

CHAPTER 11

A Modern City Emerges
1945–1960

The postwar period was a boom time for Montreal in terms of the city's population, economy, and size. The period was spent making up for lost time, after the hardships of depression and war. It was also a time when a strong desire to modernize swept across a broad range of areas.

Expansion

Rapid postwar growth was first felt in the raw numbers. Between 1941 and 1961, the Montreal census metropolitan area (CMA) grew by nearly one million people, up from 1,140,000 to 2,110,000. The city itself reached the milestone of one million inhabitants in 1951, but people were flocking mainly to the suburbs.

These figures can be explained by a sharp spike in births, the baby boom. Montreal in the 1950s was a city where children were everywhere: on the streets, in the lanes, and in parks and schools. Immigration then picked up again—fuelled by economic difficulties in postwar Europe—and continued practically unabated for the next 15 years. At first, the new wave brought British immigrants and European refugees to the city, followed by large numbers of Italians and

Greeks. The age-old tradition of people moving from the countryside to the city had been slowed by the depression, but now hundreds of thousands of new residents flocked to Montreal from all across the province.

All these migrants were naturally attracted by Montreal's job prospects. And they were not disappointed as the city's economy boomed in the postwar years. The Second World War had been a shot in the arm for the manufacturing industry, and strong consumer demand, once peace had returned, made for considerably higher production and investment levels. Meanwhile, commercial and residential construction was reaching record levels.

Employment growth was even more spectacular in the services industry, be it for financial services, retailers, transportation, teaching, healthcare, or personal services. There was work for everyone, born in Montreal or otherwise, and the unemployment rate remained very low until the recession of 1957.

Montreal's economic boom came on the back of a boom for Canada as a whole, with Montreal still officially the country's largest city. It was, however, about to be overtaken by Toronto, the darling of American investment, which was growing at an even faster clip. Since the thirties, Toronto had boasted higher stock exchange transactions, while a number of insurance companies moved their headquarters from Montreal to Toronto. The upshot was that every economic indicator showed Toronto overtaking Montreal by 1960, becoming Canada's new financial centre. Montrealers took a while to realize what was going on.

The return to prosperity, which began during the war, really came into its own in the postwar years. Wages rose much faster than inflation, boosting purchasing power. More and more Montrealers could now afford the durable consumer goods they had had to do without for years: a fridge, a car, a modern place to live. They embraced consumer society, a phenomenon that would become more pronounced after 1960.

Montreal's rapid growth could also be seen in bricks and mortar as the city expanded every which way at once. At war's end, the city still contained vast swathes of undeveloped land annexed at the turn of the century. These became the new postwar neighbourhoods, springing up for the most part along Rivière des Prairies, also called the Back river, (Ahuntsic, Bordeaux, Cartierville) and to the east (Rosemont and Longue-Pointe), although things soon spilled over into the suburbs. On the island, some municipalities made quick progress: Saint-Michel, Montréal-Nord, and Saint-Léonard to the east; Saint-Laurent and Dorval (home to Montreal's new airport since 1941) to the west. Previously rural Île Jésus, which would become the city of Laval in 1965, also got in on the act and became more built-up around the Viau and Lachapelle bridges, while a similar phenomenon was repeated on the south shore at the foot of the Victoria and Jacques-Cartier bridges.

Cars helped the suburbs shift further and further away from downtown. The number of vehicles on the roads increased at dizzying speeds and meant suburbanites could live further away from their jobs. All of which was not without problems. Traffic got heavier and parking more difficult; drivers lamented the lack of highways and bridges. In the late 1950s, the construction of Métropolitain boulevard and the Laurentides expressway brought relief, but massive investment in the regional expressway grid would come in the following two decades.

The new postwar suburb brought with it a number of changes to life in Montreal. Centred around the car, it helped bring about the rise of shopping malls. Urban planning in the suburbs was different to Montreal, particularly in shifting roads away from a rectangular grid. Duplexes were still built, but bungalows were everywhere, meeting the needs of young families looking for somewhere nice to bring up their children born in the baby boom.

Urban sprawl wasn't the only result of Montreal's growth: the city centre got a makeover too. In 1945, the downtown area hadn't changed much since the late twenties as construction had stalled due to the depression and war, but new projects leaped off drafting tables with a vengeance in the fifties. First came the construction of Dorchester Boulevard (today Boulevard René-Lévesque) in 1954–1955. The thinking behind this was twofold: to make the business district more accessible by car and to develop a glamorous main street that would attract real estate projects. And it was along this boulevard that the biggest building of the period was built: Place Ville Marie, which opened in 1962. Its modern architecture soon made it the poster child for a new era. Other skyscrapers sprouted up around it, making Dorchester the backbone of the new downtown area that would soon supplant Old Montreal as the place to do business. Even though this new world became especially visible after 1960, it was already in the works in the 1950s, when Montreal's modernization was planned.

Winds of change

The postwar period saw strong winds of change gust across Montreal society. The strongest desire for change came from the new French-Canadian middle class. Expanding in the 1920s, it had been given a rough ride by the depression, but the return to prosperity had it back up on its feet. Professionals, small business owners, insurance agents, and the like all benefited from a richer French-Canadian clientele that was swelling in numbers before their very eyes. These professionals played a key role at the Chamber of Commerce and other organizations that had a stake in the debates over Quebec's future.

New professionals such as economists, labour relations specialists, social workers, and psychologists were also making up a growing share of Montreal's elite. As in the twenties, university professors like François-Albert Angers, Michel Brunet, and Pierre Elliott Trudeau ventured onto the public stage. Montreal's unions saw new leaders emerge, and the likes of Gérard Picard, Claude Jodoin, Roger Provost, and Louis Laberge quickly became household names.

The media was another vector of change, especially CBC/Radio-Canada's television station, which started broadcasting in 1952. Its news programs opened the eyes of Montrealers and put them in touch with the world of culture. Radio, television, and newspaper journalists—the Judith Jasmins, André Laurendeaus, and René Lévesques of the province—became stars and made a huge contribution to shaping public opinion.

The world of education was also a harbinger of change. Even though French Canadians had done less schooling than English-speaking Canadians, the levels attained were on the rise from one generation to the next, as demonstrated by the expanding high school and vocational training sectors. For part of the French-Canadian population, education had become synonymous with social mobility. Nothing symbolized this better than the classical colleges—which grew in leaps and bounds. Many new colleges opened in Montreal and older ones expanded to meet demand.

Montreal society after the war had a real hunger for modernization. This desire was expressed by a group of artists led

A BOULEVARD TO A NEW ERA

Completed in 1955, Dorchester (now René-Lévesque) boulevard was
constructed to provide an easier automobile access to the new Central
Business District. It ran parallel to Sainte-Catherine (on the right) helping
alleviate the traffic on that major artery. In the span of a few years, the
boulevard would be lined with brand new skyscrapers. These would dwarf
the Sun Life Building (centre of the photo), which had dominated the
urban landscape since the 1930s.

(Archives de la Ville de Montréal, R3165-1-2-060)

by Paul-Émile Borduas in the *Refus global* manifesto of 1948, but it was also increasingly prevalent among the new French-Canadian elites as people looked for a counterbalance to the traditionalism of the Church and the Duplessis government by calling for greater freedom of thought and profound social and political reforms. With new means of communication and travel now easier, Montrealers also now had first-hand knowledge of what Americans were up to, and the United States became a model to be followed.

This desire for change ran up against resistance from the Church, which remained on the defensive. Religious observance was on the wane in Montreal, especially among the working class. Moral standards were harder to uphold given the rise in modern communications and new social and cultural practices in a diversifying society. The Church was unable to cope with rising demands in education, hospital care, and social services and increasingly had to turn to secular staff, who were wary of the control the priests and nuns exerted over them. The episcopate of Archbishop Joseph Charbonneau (1940–1950) nevertheless gave lay workers an opportunity to become more involved in the Church's endeavours. The archbishop proved willing to adapt the Church to the new realities of a modern, cosmopolitan city, but the Church in Montreal hardened under Paul-Émile Léger, who was appointed archbishop in 1950 and a cardinal in 1953 and who sought to exercise the Church's authority in a manner more in line with tradition. This position was untenable in the long term, and by the late fifties Cardinal Léger had softened the Church's stance and started a dialogue that would overhaul its role in the wake of the Quiet Revolution and Vatican II.

The winds of change blowing over Montreal did not affect just the Church. French-speaking elites grew increasingly uncomfortable with the second-class status of French Canadians in their own city. The privileged position of English Canadians was perceived to be the cause. Anger mounted at the influence of the English language in Montreal life, given the bilingualism imposed only on French Canadians and the fact that many organizations and businesses used only English in their dealings with French-speaking customers. Discontent also rumbled on due to the discrimination against French Canadians on the job market, where they were paid less and had problems being promoted and moving into senior management. The "Château Maisonneuve" scandal of 1954–1955 stoked the fires of resentment when the president of the Canadian National Railways refused to reconsider his decision to call the new hotel his company was having built "The Queen Elizabeth." And tensions went up another notch in 1955 when the suspension of Canadiens hockey star Maurice Richard was taken to be a national affront, sparking the Richard Riot. The anger among French Canadians would come to a head in the 1960s.

The political battlefield

The political scene was not spared the winds of change. Since 1940, Montreal had been living under a new regime that had set democracy back on its heels. With 99 city councillors divided into three categories and a third of them unelected, municipal politics had become a complex affair, a battlefield for varying interests. Various clans on the city council sought to broaden their influence and more than anything hoped to be represented on the executive committee, the real seat of power. They cobbled together alliances and relied on give and take to pursue their agendas and access the system of patronage that was the crux of political life. In spite of everything,

HE SHOOTS, HE SCORES

Since its first game, in 1910, the Canadien Hockey Club has been a
fundamental component of Montreal's soul. The team has won a total of
24 Stanley Cups. The Forum was its home arena from 1926 to 1996, when
the team moved to the Bell Centre. During the 1950s, the local hero was
Maurice "The Rocket" Richard, who scored more goals than any other
player of his time. In 1955, his suspension provoked a revolt of his fans
known as the Forum Riot or the Maurice Richard Riot.

(Les éditions du Septentrion, Journal *La Presse*)

"Monsieur Montréal" Camillien Houde, who won back the mayoralty from 1944 to 1954, and J.-O. Asselin, chairman of the executive committee from 1940 to 1954, steadied the ship.

A wave of reform, stirred by an investigation into public morality, rose up in the early 1950s. Pacifique (Pax) Plante, a lawyer and the former assistant head of the Montreal police department, set the ball rolling when he was relieved of his duties in 1948. In a tell-all series of newspaper articles later published as a pamphlet, *Montreal sous le règne de la pègre* (Montreal in the grips of the underworld), Plante exposed the extent to which prostitution and illegal gambling permeated Montreal life—and the blind eye police officers and politicians turned to such activities, making Montreal an "open city" where anything went. A number of associations joined forces to form a public morality committee and successfully called for a public inquiry into police activities, chaired by Judge François Caron. Pacifique Plante played a key role in proceedings, along with a young lawyer by the name of Jean Drapeau. From 1950 to 1954, Judge Caron called witnesses and wrote up a report that confirmed Plante's claims and condemned a string of police officers.

As in 1909–1910, the corruption scandal led to a cleanup. Politicians were tainted by the scandal and Mayor Houde chose to retire from political life. Flushed with success after his role in the Caron inquiry, Jean Drapeau ran for mayor. He became head of the Civic Action League (Ligue d'action civique), a political party he had created with city councillor Pierre DesMarais. It was the first time a true political party had appeared on the municipal scene, which had been dominated until then by loose groupings of independent councillors. In the 1954 election, Drapeau won the mayoral race and his party was rewarded with a sizable number of seats on the city council, if not a majority. With the backing of the Category

THE DOWNTOWN BEAT IN 1961
By the 1960s, the former uptown area had become the new downtown
where the big corporations moved their offices, abandoning Old Montreal.
Sainte-Catherine was more than ever the liveliest street in town, with its
numerous stores, movie palaces, restaurants, and cafés.

(Archives de la Ville de Montréal, VM94-A27-010)

C unelected councillors, the League took control of the executive committee, with DesMarais as chairman.

The League's opponents learned from the experience and formed their own party, the Ralliement du Grand Montréal (Greater Montreal Rally). They were supported by the Union nationale, which had a score or two to settle with Drapeau, a prominent opponent of Premier Maurice Duplessis. In the elections of 1957, the Ralliement du Grand Montréal managed to have Sarto Fournier elected as mayor. The party won fewer seats on the council than the Civic Action League, but took a leaf out of Drapeau's book to earn the support of the Category C councillors and obtained the chairmanship of the executive committee.

Throughout this period, since neither group enjoyed a majority of seats, the city council became a real battlefield where opposing clans clashed. Even the most straightforward of projects would lead to endless debate, paralyzing the city's administration. Elections, in 1957 especially, were held before a backdrop of violence. The city appeared to have become ungovernable, particularly between 1957 and 1960, which explains the sea change that occurred in 1960.

That year saw Montrealers decide in a referendum to do away with Category C city councillors. Henceforth the council would be made up of 66 elected officials, half Category A (elected by property owners alone), half Category B (elected by owners and tenants alike).

Jean Drapeau chose this moment to make his comeback. Shortly before the elections, he set up a new political party, the Parti civique (the Civic Party). He offered voters the chance to breathe new life into municipal politics by electing a majority government to put an end to the squabbles that had paralyzed the council in previous years. Montrealers were indeed disgusted with a situation that had prevailed since 1957

A NEW LANDMARK FOR MONTREAL

Place Ville Marie is an office building complex dominated by a cross-shaped 44-storey tower. New York developer William Zeckendorf was the driving force behind this project with his architects, I. M. Pei & Associates. Construction began in 1958 and the inauguration took place in 1962. Place Ville Marie instantly became the symbol of modern architecture in Montreal and was recognized as a city landmark.

(Archives de la Ville de Montréal, VM94-A365-011)

and voiced their discontent by electing Drapeau mayor and awarding two thirds of seats to Civic Party councillors.

It was quite the turnaround. With a clear majority in the council, Drapeau had six councillors from his own party elected to the executive committee. As with the National Assembly in Quebec City and Parliament in Ottawa, Montreal would now be managed by an administration formed entirely by members of the party that held the majority. The city enjoyed unprecedented levels of unity and efficiency.

In the hectic politics of the postwar years, various issues monopolized public opinion. One of them—the management of public utilities by private businesses—was resolved at last. Since the turn of the century, a number of groups had periodically campaigned for the nationalization of public utilities. Electricity was the first when in 1944 the Quebec government acquired Montreal Light, Heat, and Power to form Hydro-Québec. Then, in 1951, it was the turn of the tramway company that was replaced by the Commission de transport de Montréal or the Montreal Transportation Commission, a public body dominated by the City of Montreal, although the suburbs were also represented. The Commission oversaw the systematic replacement of tramways by buses, a process that ended in 1959.

Another hot-button issue was the ability of municipalities on the island of Montreal to work together, a matter of greater urgency since the city's suburbs had taken off after the war. There was much discussion of regionalizing some services that were provided by each municipality. But there was great distrust between Montreal and its suburbs. The Commission métropolitaine de Montréal—Montreal Metropolitan Commission—had been up and running since 1921, but its powers were limited. It was replaced in 1959 by the Corporation du Montréal métropolitain (Montreal Metropolitan Corporation), with the city centre and suburbs each having an equal number of seats and its chair appointed by the government of Quebec. The corporation was scarcely more efficient than its predecessor, however, and it was not until 1970 that the issue of the regional management of certain municipal services was settled once and for all.

Much debate was also devoted to urban renewal in the 1950s. Slums in the older neighbourhoods of Montreal were regularly denounced, but no solution to the problem could be agreed on. In 1954, a major renewal project, the Dozois Plan, proposed demolishing many of the slums near downtown Montreal and replacing them with affordable housing. The plan was debated endlessly, with disagreement over whether to turn this part of the city into a residential neighbourhood or a business district and what type of buildings there would be. In spite of the opposition, Habitations Jeanne-Mance were at last built in the area between de Montigny (now Maisonneuve) and Ontario street to the east of Saint-Laurent boulevard, but represented a very limited response to the problem posed by rundown housing in the city.

For politics and society as a whole, the postwar years paved the way for the Quiet Revolution and the sweeping changes it would bring. Growing prosperity led to grander aspirations and a hunger for change that would be satisfied after 1960.

CHAPTER 12

Fireworks
1960–1976

The Swinging Sixties were a particularly lively time in Montreal, with the excitement of the Quiet Revolution and the most modern of makeovers for the city. Expo 67 only added to the fever. All this excitement nevertheless masked the slide towards economic slowdown and a demographic downturn that even the 1976 Olympics could not conceal.

Building the Montreal of the future

Throughout the Western world, the 1960s were abuzz with excitement, and Montreal was naturally no exception. Young people around the world began to stand up for themselves, traditional models were thrown into question, and new-found freedoms were exploited to the hilt. The age-old battle between old and new again reared its head, this time with modernity coming out on top.

In Quebec, the phenomenon was magnified by the Quiet Revolution, which began in 1960. Swept in by winds of liberation and national affirmation, the Quiet Revolution sought to make up for lost time in a number of clearly identified areas. In Montreal, the resurgence of French Canadians sparked the political and cultural upheavals we will examine below.

LES NUITS DE MONTRÉAL

Montreal's nightlife is renowned throughout North America. Sainte-Catherine Street (photographed here in 1964) was the epicentre of the city's show business. It attracted not only Montrealers but also a growing number of tourists, especially Americans.

(Archives de la Ville de Montréal, VM94-A144-026_1)

Increased government intervention born of the Quiet Revolution played a major role in modernizing the economy and life in general in Montreal. The Quebec government, supported by Ottawa, launched the construction of a vast network of highways and bridges that would be completed over the following decade. It invested in new administrative buildings (including a new courthouse), along with new schools, university buildings, and other public buildings. For its part, the federal government planned to build the administrative building that became the Complexe Guy-Favreau and the CBC/Radio-Canada tower.

The modernization of Montreal owed much to Jean Drapeau, mayor throughout the sixties and seventies. A man of vision and ambitious projects, Drapeau had big plans for Montreal and its role and influence abroad. He started work on the Métro, which was inaugurated in 1966. He supported the promoters who wanted to develop the new downtown along recently widened Dorchester boulevard (now René-Lévesque). Place Ville Marie, an imposing skyscraper opened in 1962, was the jewel in the crown—and the starting point for the underground city—but many more complexes were added in the space of a few years. They had an equally modern shine and completely transformed the cityscape around them.

All this construction work did away with thousands of homes and shifted their occupants elsewhere, putting the spotlight on housing and leading to political repercussions. Part of Montreal's history fell at the hands of the demolition experts, as thoughts had not yet turned to preserving the city's heritage.

Montreal's mayor nevertheless had very little control over another aspect of the city's transformation: urban sprawl. In 1961, "his" city was home to 56 percent of the Montreal area population, a figure that had shrunk to 39 percent 15 years later. Cars were quite clearly the driving force behind the new suburbs, which were given a boost as new bridges went up and more highways were built. The suburbs were increasingly expanding off the island of Montreal and were home to almost one million people in 1976.

But Jean Drapeau's greatest success was bringing the 1967 International and Universal Exposition to Montreal. It was a moment to remember for all Montrealers who, for six months, were able to discover the world around them in all its glory. Expo 67 also sped up construction work on the Métro and highways, and Mayor Drapeau was keen to repeat the feat by organizing the 1976 Olympic Games. This time, however, the event was a sporting success, but had very little impact on urban development. Worse, it had a negative effect: the sky-high costs of building the Olympic Stadium bled the city's finances dry and put an end to Mayor Drapeau's out-of-the-box thinking.

Expo 67 gave Montrealers illusions of grandeur just as their city was beginning to slide. Experts predicted close to five million people would be living in Montreal and the surrounding area by 1981, but in reality there were less than three million. So what happened?

Reorganizing the economy

Throughout the 1960s, the model Montreal's economic development had been built on for more than a century began to crumble.

It was largely based on making the most of Montreal's ideal positioning as a crossroads for trade between Canada and the United Kingdom. But for decades trade between the two countries had been declining, as Canada focused more on the United States market. The coup de grâce came in 1973, when the U.K. joined the European Common Market.

EXPO 67

"Man and his World" was the unifying theme of the international exhibition held
in Montreal in 1967. The event took place in the middle of the St. Lawrence River,
on islands that had been artificially enlarged for the occasion, using earth and rock
excavated for the construction of the Métro system. The site was exceptional. On
the right side of the photo is the last segment of the St. Lawrence Seaway, a joint
Canadian-American undertaking, completed in 1959.

(Ville de Montréal, Collection Claude Bouchard)

The model was also built around impressive manufacturing output destined for the Canadian market and protected from competition abroad by high customs duties. But international agreements whittled away at this protection and enabled emerging countries to supplant Canadian production in low-paying industries. Businesses that made consumer goods—so important to Montreal—felt the pinch. Moreover, Montreal factories were old and companies that chose to modernize and concentrate production often moved to Ontario.

Montreal was further disadvantaged by losing its status as Canada's largest city. By around 1960, Toronto had crept ahead of Montreal by most measures, apart from number of inhabitants (which would come about in 1976), with the gap between the two cities continuing to widen throughout the sixties and seventies. The rise of a new form of Quebec nationalism came at a time when Montreal's economy was well on its way to unravelling and, although it accelerated the process, it was not the underlying cause. Several big businesses moved their headquarters to Toronto, which was quickly becoming the country's undisputed leader and was now at the very heart of its financial system. This came as a severe blow to Montreal, which lost tens of thousands of residents and well-paid jobs.

The pace of growth was feeling the effects by 1967: private investment was running out of steam, and there were fewer immigrants just when Quebec's birth rate plummeted. The city's population reached new heights with 1,214,352 inhabitants in 1966, before, for the first time in the history of Montreal, falling back, to 1,080,546 in 1976. The suburbs did continue to grow, but at a slower pace than before, and the entire Montreal census metropolitan area attracted scarcely more than 50,000 newcomers between 1971 and 1976, settling at 2,802,485.

Despite the slowdown, it was still a time of prosperity for most Montrealers as the postwar rise in living standards continued throughout the sixties and seventies.

One reason for this improvement was a jump in the number of skilled workers, who commanded better wages as a result. Education levels were on the rise in general, and vocational training became more comprehensive. A second factor was the growing number of women taking to the workforce, which boosted the number of two-income households.

The Quiet Revolution and the development of the welfare state in general also helped raise living standards. Putting in place an extensive network of social and medical services and expanding education services also saw the quality of the services improve in leaps and bounds compared to the 1950s. Government intervention was also noticeable in terms of increased public investment.

French-speaking Montrealers take control of the city

One of the most significant aspects of Montreal's development after 1960 was without a doubt what became known as the "reconquest of Montreal." This reconquest was fuelled by the Quiet Revolution and by a new Quebec nationalism that questioned the power wielded by an English-Canadian minority over many facets of life in Quebec, especially in Montreal.

Montreal was a focal point for the rise of nationalism in Quebec, both strategically and symbolically, since the English language was more visible, and audible, and the fault lines between those who spoke French and English were more clearly drawn than elsewhere: while many of Quebec's regions were almost exclusively French speaking, French was the mother tongue of only 65 percent of people in the Montreal area. It was therefore no great surprise to see Montrealers actively involved in the struggles of the nationalist movement and playing a key role first in the rise of the independence movement with the Rassemblement pour l'indépendance nationale (1960–1968), then in the rise of the sovereignty movement with the Parti québécois, founded in 1968. General de Gaulle chose none other than the balcony of Montreal's City Hall to cry "*Vive le Québec libre!*" in 1967, and throughout the sixties and seventies, various nationalist demonstrations were held in the city. Some—notably the Saint-Jean-Baptiste celebrations in 1968 and the protests for a "McGill *français*"—turned violent.

It was in Montreal that the terrorist activities of the Front de libération du Québec were concentrated, there that bombs were planted between 1963 and 1970, there that the October Crisis of 1970 took place, as British diplomat James Richard Cross and Quebec labour minister Pierre Laporte were kidnapped (the latter losing his life). The October Crisis was significant for the reactions it provoked, at the municipal level, where Mayor Drapeau made one alarmist statement after the other, and also at the provincial and, especially, federal levels. Pierre Elliott Trudeau's government proclaimed the War Measures Act and sent the army to Montreal, which quickly looked like a city under siege. The hundreds of arrests made in the city looked beyond the FLQ and aimed to crush both the nationalist movement and left-wing groups. The strategy ultimately ended in failure, however, as trade unions and the sovereignty movement grew stronger in the seventies. For both, Montreal remained a hotbed of social and political change, and French-speaking masses in the city played an important role in bringing the Parti québécois to power in 1976.

Most of the linguistic battles of the sixties played out in Montreal. Until then, public signage in Montreal had been, at best, bilingual and most often in English only. The tendency for minority ethnic groups and immigrants to adopt English had also made great headway. The nationalist reaction was triggered in particular by the Saint-Léonard schools crisis, which pitted Italian immigrants opposed to a requirement to study in French against French Canadians, eventually leading successive Quebec governments to pass a series of language laws (Bills 63, 22, and 101) to reinforce the status of the French language in Quebec. The effects would be felt for years to come.

One of the goals of the Quiet Revolution was to ensure that French Canadians could access key posts in Quebec's economy and society as a whole. The goal was first met as the state apparatus grew in size, before attention focused on the private sector. Businesses run by English Canadians and foreign companies made room for French-speaking executives among their Quebec management from the 1970s on, bringing an end to decades of discrimination. More remarkable still was the rise of a new French-speaking business elite that reached leading positions in Montreal's economy.

As the city was becoming even more French, women were also involved in another important struggle of their own. The rebirth of the feminist movement in the sixties was not unique to Montreal—it was sweeping across the West—but the battle for equality and independence affected many areas of life in Montreal: legal status, access to political power, the workforce and trade unions, financial independence, and the right to contraception and abortion, among others. Montreal felt the full force of this phenomenon more than anywhere else in Quebec: it was there that the more militant groups met, there that the biggest demonstrations were held. In this respect, as in so many others, Montreal was Quebec's social laboratory, the place where the bells of change were being rung the hardest.

The period that began in 1960 was characterized by profound social change, fostered by the peculiar climate of the Quiet Revolution and postwar prosperity. These transformations took on an international dimension that was visible in the new values emerging and were powered by a "youth phenomenon" as the baby-boom generation reached adulthood. Across Quebec and in Montreal, one of the most striking aspects of these changes was the rewriting of the Church's role in the wake of Vatican II and the clergy's withdrawal from society, the result of the Quiet Revolution. Cardinal Léger's stepping down in 1967 as archbishop of Montreal and subsequent departure for Cameroon well and truly marked the end of an era.

A cultural revival

All this social and political change was set against a backdrop of cultural vitality. Quebec culture had been revived. Resolutely modern and outward looking, it shouted its intentions from the rooftops in the sixties. Authors—like Hubert Aquin, Jacques Godbout, Gaston Miron, and Michel Tremblay—movie directors, singers, actors, musicians, painters, and sculptors worked for the most part out of Montreal, helping shape its new identity. Concert halls (particularly the Place des Arts complex), bigger and better museums, bookstores, and galleries made it all available to the public.

Most of note here is the pivotal role that Montreal played as the hotbed of Quebec culture, both in terms of creativity and showcasing this cultural revival. The city was home to the major French-language television networks, along with the performing arts companies and publishing houses. Artists from all over Quebec were working in Montreal. With its four universities (Université de Montréal, McGill, Université du

Québec à Montréal, and Concordia) and its research centres, the city was abuzz with creativity and scientific discovery.

Montreal intellectuals fuelled the fire of ideas raging across the whole province with comments and essays, while magazines like *Liberté* and *Parti pris* had considerable influence in their respective milieux, as did *The Last Post* in English.

And the city lit up the imaginations of its artists. With *Les Belles-Sœurs* (1968), Michel Tremblay brought *joual*, the language of working-class Montrealers, to the stage with a bang. Beau Dommage sang about the Montreal experience to great success, and huge numbers of novelists, movie directors, photographers, painters, and sculptors drew on the city for inspiration.

Montreal was also a crossroads where Quebec creations met foreign influences, especially ones from south of the border. Robert Charlebois, for instance, put words straight from the mouth of many a Montrealer to a very American style of music, and took his message and style all the way to France. And cultural productions from all around the world were given a warm welcome on the Montreal market.

Montreal's English-language cultural scene also remained lively during the 1960s, despite the fact that Toronto had come to dominate English-Canadian culture. Montrealers such as singer-songwriter Leonard Cohen, poet Irving Layton, and author Mordecai Richler found in their city a powerful inspiration.

Modernizing politics

In municipal politics, 1960 marked a real break with the politics of the fifties. This new political scene was dominated by the personality of Jean Drapeau, mayor from 1960 to 1986, and by the Parti civique that he led. A new regime and a new style of government came to City Hall. The Parti civique had a majority on the council and could govern the city by holding all the seats on the executive committee. Drapeau was very popular indeed in the 1960s. He and executive committee chairman Lucien Saulnier formed one of the strongest teams in the city's history, and he was able to reform the way the city was governed and to find solutions to problems posed by issues like traffic, parking, and inadequate public facilities.

The Drapeau administration encouraged projects to modernize the city, but it was severely criticized for turning a blind eye to the people forced to move out of their homes by demolition and its limited efforts to build new housing. It also had scant regard for what the decline of industry was doing to Montreal.

Starting in the late 1960s, the Parti civique came up against stiff opposition, mainly from citizens' groups in poor neighbourhoods and from trade union organizers. Its opponents leaned left, covering the spectrum between social democracy and Marxism-Leninism, and called for radical changes to how the city was governed and how it dealt with its citizens. First grouped together in 1970 under the banner of the short-lived Front d'action politique (FRAP), the administration's opponents set up the RCM, the Rassemblement des citoyens de Montréal (Montreal Citizens' Movement) in 1974.

Another aspect of a more modern political scene in Montreal was the emergence of a metropolitan level of government, an issue that had divided representatives of the city and its suburbs for years. A solution was at last found in 1970, with the creation of the Communauté urbaine de Montréal, or the Montreal Urban Community (CUM). The CUM took charge of various municipal services, notably policing, public transit, realty assessments, urban development plans, and cleaning up the city's air and water. Its creation spread the financial burden of these services more evenly.

So were Expo 67 and the 1976 Olympics nothing more than an impressive fireworks display? The changes made to Montreal after 1960 were all in the spirit of modernization, but they led to major upheavals and the city had a hard time adjusting. Montreal lost ground to other cities in Canada and was further weakened by departures for Toronto. Revitalized by a new French-speaking elite, Montreal remained a vibrant place to live and work, but its future didn't look so bright in 1976.

MAJOR LEAGUE BASEBALL

Baseball had long been played in Montréal—Jackie Robinson began his professional career here—but the city had to wait until 1969 to attract a major league team. The Montreal Expos played in the National League until 2004 when the franchise was moved to Washington, D. C. During the first years, the team had its local games at Jarry Park; in 1977, it moved to the brand new Olympic Stadium. This photo, taken on May 31, 1991, shows Ivan Calderon in action.

(Archives de la Ville de Montréal)

CHAPTER 13

Difficult Days
1976–1994

In the 1970s, Montreal entered a long period of weak growth and economic restructuring. Dark, gloomy clouds settled over the city. But, in spite of everything, it continued to be renowned around the world for its cultural vitality. Montrealers and their leaders relaunched Quebec's leading city, building on its inner strengths and heritage.

A long adjustment

The years 1976 to 1994 were testing times for the city's economy. The city was shaken by recessions in 1981–1982 and 1990–1992. Unemployment rates were the highest in decades. Things were particularly bad in the older parts of town, where most welfare recipients lived, and better in the suburbs. But the problems weren't due to the whims of the economy alone: they were worsened by major changes to Montreal's economy.

Rethinking the economic structure that had characterized Montreal since the mid-nineteenth century had a huge impact on the city in the seventies and eighties. Many manufacturing industries that had once been a big part of life in the city—the shoe, textile, and garment industries—were in decline, and a large number of companies were having to shut down or slash employee numbers because production was shifting towards developing countries, where wages were much lower. Heavy industry also met with stiff competition from abroad, and advances in technology worked against Montreal too, since its factories were old and sometimes outdated. Production of rolling stock—a victim of the decline of the railways—was a shadow of its former self, while refineries and many other factories were dismantled.

Montreal's traditional role as Canada's transportation hub also took a beating. Vancouver emerged as the country's biggest port, thanks to closer trade ties between Canada and Pacific-rim countries, although container ships reinvented Montreal's port as an important stop on the North Atlantic axis. New handling facilities went up in the city's east end, but there were far fewer longshoremen than before and the Old Port was abandoned before becoming a tourist destination. The decline of rail transportation in favour of trucks and buses reduced activity in a sector that had once been a mainstay of Montreal's economy. As for air transportation, Montreal had taken less than a decade to tumble from its dominant position in the early sixties as Toronto rose to become the country's main hub for national and international air traffic. The opening of an international airport in Mirabel (1975)—which ended up a real white elephant—made things worse still, since dividing activities between two airports robbed Montreal of its role as a transit and connecting point.

The decline of traditional industries was not unique to Montreal and affected many cities along the eastern seaboard of the United States at the same time. In many sectors, businesses managed to survive by moving to more modern facilities, but many moved to Ontario, a province closer to the heart of the Canadian market. When they did decide to remain in Montreal, many opted to move to the suburbs, near

the highways. The result was the rapid and massive deindus-
trialization of the city's manufacturing areas, particularly
along the Lachine Canal and in the Hochelaga-Maisonneuve
district.

But it was not all gloom and doom. Montreal and the surrounding area enjoyed major investments in cutting-edge
industries like aeronautics, pharmaceuticals, and information
technologies; companies hired skilled workers who commanded higher salaries than in traditional sectors; and many
small- and medium-sized businesses sprang up, specializing
in exports. In all, Montreal emerged from the process with
considerably more modern, and more efficient, manufacturing facilities. They employed only a small percentage of the
working population, however, and industrial reorganization
left thousands of workers without jobs, workers who had a
tough time learning new trades.

One major aspect of the transformation of the Montreal
economy was the space taken up by the services sector. This
sector included retail stores, firms specializing in consulting
engineering, accounting and law, major advertising and travel
agencies, financial services firms, psychologists, restaurants,
public and para-public utilities, people in the performing arts,
broadcasters, and more. This diverse collection of services
employed the bulk of Montreal's workforce.

Many head offices moving to Toronto also led to the loss
of a considerable number of administrative employees, com-
pensated—but only in part—by the emergence of big French-
language businesses like Provigo, Bombardier, and Quebecor,
and of government-owned companies like Hydro-Québec
and the Caisse de dépôt et placement du Québec. Headquartered in Montreal, these companies added to the city's
financial health. The mergers and acquisitions movement
concentrated economic power in Montreal, making it more

than ever Quebec's economic and financial driver, the place where the big decisions were made. The decision by a number of big Canadian companies—the likes of Alcan, BCE, and Power Corporation—to keep their headquarters in Montreal also helped ensure Montreal remained one of Canada's leading cities and boosted its standing abroad.

Urban sprawl

Needless to say, the disruptions to Montreal's economy were reflected in slower population growth. Throughout this period (1976–94), the population of the city itself hovered around one million people. Population figures for the Montreal census metropolitan area rose from 2.8 million in 1976 to 3.3 million in 1996, but the area had also grown. An increase of 500,000 people in 20 years is remarkably little, especially when compared to Toronto, where the gain was three times higher.

A number of factors were responsible for Montreal's population stagnation. First, there was the drop-off in the birth rate, particularly after 1965, which contrasted with the baby boom of the previous period. Then, the centuries-old tradition of moving from the countryside to the city slowed. Farmers were now few and far between in Quebec, and the people who lived in villages and small towns found the bright city lights less appealing. To add to its woes, Montreal lost a good number of its residents to other cities in Canada, Toronto especially.

International immigration partly made up for these departures, although a smaller proportion of people immigrating to Canada were now settling in Montreal. People born abroad still made up some 15 percent of those living in the Montreal area, and that percentage would be greater still if it included their children born in Canada.

Aside from a slowdown in growth, the most striking phenomenon is how the population was spread across the Montreal area. Montreal's share declined as the city lost out to its suburbs: in 1996, the city had only 30 percent of the total. The suburbs experienced a huge rise, building on their previous numbers. In the sixties, it was the extreme east and west of the island, along with Île Jésus (which became the city of Laval in 1965) that reaped the rewards, but over the following two decades, most newcomers settled on the north and south shores. By the early nineties, Montreal and the surrounding area boasted some 130 municipalities.

Mainly young French-speaking families moved to the suburbs in search of reasonably priced housing and somewhere quieter to bring up their children, following in the footsteps of English families. For the time being, however, few people from recent immigrant families made the move.

The suburbs were far from uniform and, as in other parts of Montreal, there were considerable differences between the upper-class and poorer neighbourhoods. A dependency on getting around by car was one common feature, heightened by an increase in local shopping malls, with a gradual shift away from bedroom suburbs where residents commuted to and from the downtown area morning and evening. Companies set up shop in these new towns, creating a host of service jobs and reducing dependency on the city centre. In the long term, this urban sprawl raised tricky questions about how to coordinate and plan the metropolitan area, since all these municipalities were competing with each other to attract new investment. By the late 1980s, the need for greater regional dialogue was a frequent bone of contention.

A French-speaking, multi-ethnic city

The reconquest of Montreal reached its peak at the very start of this period (1976–1994). Quebec's National Assembly adopted the Charter of the French Language (Bill 101) in 1977, putting an end to a decade of language disputes, with Montreal being at the heart of them. Montreal's streets were transformed by the introduction of French-only commercial signs and advertisements. There was also a sea change in education, where the children of immigrants had to attend French-language schools, thus overturning long-standing trends. The movement also affected the workplace, where French became more widespread. Meanwhile, big Canadian and foreign businesses began to appoint French-speaking executives to head Quebec operations as a matter of course.

Montrealers of French origin continued to make up a little less than two thirds of the population living in the city and surrounding area. The decision by some to move to the suburbs reduced their share on the island of Montreal, where only 55 percent of residents claimed to have French as their mother tongue in 1996.

Meanwhile, Montrealers of British stock, whose relative share had been fading for more than a century, also saw their absolute numbers drop off from the 1970s onwards, the result of so many leaving for Toronto, fewer immigrants arriving from the United Kingdom, and a drop in birthrate. English-speaking Montrealers now included people from different backgrounds, following language shifts that affected groups who had been in the city for quite a while, notably many Ashkenazi Jews, Italians, and Greeks.

But the biggest phenomenon of all was the surge in the population whose mother tongue was neither French nor English, the result of radical changes in migration patterns.

Until the sixties, most immigrants came to Montreal from Europe, but then changes to Canada's immigration policy welcomed people from anywhere in the world. From the seventies, most of these new immigrants to Montreal came from Asia, the Caribbean, Latin America, and North Africa. Ethnic diversity arrived in Montreal in a very big way. By 1996, one third of people living in and around the city had neither French nor British ancestry, making Montreal the only place of its kind in Quebec.

And so, just as French regained its place of honour in the city, Montreal was also becoming more multicultural. Up until 1960, the old compartmental strategy in the city had meant that each ethnic group had developed away from the others, but barriers began to come down in the seventies, with Montreal's ethnic diversity acknowledged and even celebrated. Saint-Laurent boulevard, traditionally at the heart of the city's corridor for immigration, came to symbolize, more than anywhere else, Montreal in all its diversity. Crowds thronged there, looking for a taste of the exotic or eager to strengthen ties with their culture of origin.

Taking back the city

The adventure of the Olympic Games in 1976 put an end to an age of grand projects and Montreal's reckless pursuit of modernization at any cost. Resistance put up by citizens' committees and the general public showed that the city could no longer do away with islands of greenery and throw hundreds of tenants out on the street with impunity.

Groups were also mustering, especially as of 1973, to defend the city's built heritage. At first concerned at the fate awaiting the houses built in the heyday of the Anglo-Protestant elite, these groups came to adopt a broader attitude to heritage, including industrial sites, neighbourhoods, and the urban environment. They managed to make Montrealers aware of the need to preserve the heritage around them. Demolitions were a thing of the past: preserving, restoring, and renovating was now very much in vogue. The city offered financial assistance to owners who wanted to repair their homes, hopeful that public-housing projects would fit into the existing urban fabric, rather than try to replace it.

The city also tried to revitalize older neighbourhoods, by reviving shopping streets, opening new cultural centres, and replacing lamp posts, fire hydrants, and the like. A big part of Montreal's revitalization came by breathing life back into its neighbourhoods.

Cultural venues for the city and surrounding area also proliferated, and were visited by more and more Montrealers. The biggest museums expanded, while others opened. New theatre and dance companies were set up in renovated old buildings. The Olympic Vélodrome became the Biodôme. Tourist attractions like Old Montreal and the Old Port were given fresh appeal, drawing millions of visitors every year and featuring a broad range of cultural activities.

All this was possible because Montreal had become a hotbed of cultural creativity, Quebec's main showcase for fresh, French-language culture that was uniquely *Made in Québec*. Now backed more than ever by all layers of government, this culture was also able to make its voice heard through Montreal-based newspapers, electronic media, publishing houses, and more.

Montrealers taking back their own city could also be seen in increasingly creative—and popular—festivals, some of which took to the city's streets. The Montreal International Jazz Festival, Just for Laughs, Les Francofolies, the World Film Festival, and more put on a show for all the world to see, despite a lingering feeling of economic gloom. Pride in the city hit a high note in 1992, during the festivities marking Montreal's 350th anniversary. The celebrations included the opening of Pointe-à-Callière, a museum devoted to Montreal's history and archaeology.

These facilities and cultural events did not just have Montrealers in mind: the city was dipping its toes into international waters. Montreal showed off its worldwide credentials not with one-hit wonders, but with a string of annual events that had personalities and groups from all around the world flocking to the city. It also became one of the premier destinations in North America for international conferences, an aspect of its international side that was helped by the growth of its four universities. All this while developing ties with French-speaking countries saw Montreal cement its status as one of the premier cities in the French-speaking world, a truly international stage not only for artists and creative types, but also for internationally renowned researchers and academics.

A changing of the guard

In 1976, Mayor Jean Drapeau, head of the Parti civique, had already held the highest office in Montreal for 16 years, with 10 more to come. Although Drapeau was clearly less popular than before, a divided opposition kept him in power. As is often the case with municipal politics, parties came and went. Founded in 1974, the Rassemblement des citoyens et citoyennes de Montréal (RCM)—the Montreal Citizens' Movement—was of the longer-lasting variety, forming the official opposition after the 1974 and 1982 elections.

After the Olympic Games weakened the city's finances, the Parti civique could not govern as it had in the past. In 1978, the arrival of Yvon Lamarre as executive committee president marked a shift in party politics. Turning its back on big, expensive projects, the administration now focused on economic recovery, neighbourhood revitalization, and residential investment in an effort to slow the rate at which people were moving to the suburbs. In spite of this, the wearing effect of being in power ensured that in 1986, after holding office for 26 years at the head of the Parti civique, Drapeau retired from politics and elections swept the RCM and a new mayor, Jean Doré, to power.

Drapeau and the Parti civique were representative of the new French-speaking middle class—small storekeepers, managers, insurance agents, etc.—that had developed starting in the 1920s. Doré and the RCM represented the new elites spawned by the Quiet Revolution, made up of executives, technocrats, union leaders, and community organizers. The 1986 elections had brought a new generation to power.

For years, the RCM had said that citizens should play a bigger role in municipal politics, and, once in power, the RCM administration set up borough advisory committees and Accès-Montréal offices. It tried to get Montrealers working together, but, despite these overtures, it made the administration more technocratic, although it did continue to support a better quality of life at the local level. Mayor Doré's team was re-elected in 1990 and spent a total of eight years in power.

Throughout this period, the Communauté urbaine de Montréal was the only body to coordinate the various municipalities' efforts. Although it managed certain metropolitan services like the police and public transit, the CUM only brought together municipalities on the island of Montreal, and the city and its suburbs had grown considerably since 1970, meaning that the CUM represented a declining portion of the Montreal census metropolitan area (71% in 1971 versus 53% in 1996). The need for a broader mechanism bringing together the region's municipalities was again a talking point. Montreal underwent a long and painful period of restructuring between 1976 and 1994. Despite a vibrant cultural scene, factory closures, high unemployment, and slow growth fed a general feeling of malaise. Gradually, Montreal hauled itself out of years of crisis by banking on the knowledge economy and the quality of living in its revitalized neighbourhoods.

MONTREAL SKYLINE, WINTER 2013

Visitors to the Kondiaronk Belvédère on Mount Royal will see that the mountain still dominates the city buildings. The lookout was named after the Huron Chief, Kondiaronk, who contributed to the signing of the Great Peace of 1701.

(Photo: Robin Philpot)

CHAPTER 14

Montreal's Revival
1994...

Montreal came alive again at the turn of the twenty-first century. The doom and gloom of past decades lifted. The economy picked up and growth returned, while political reforms transformed the relationship between the city and its suburbs.

A new economic boom

In 1994, Montreal's economy was still reeling from the severe recession that had struck it at the beginning of the decade. Unemployment and poverty were rife; food banks were in demand. Signs that the city was about to right the ship were, however, perceptible and would get stronger.

The long and painful process of restructuring Montreal's industry was now at an end. The city emerged with state-of-the-art businesses in cutting-edge sectors like aeronautics, biopharmaceuticals, information technologies, and telecommunications. Across the board, even in the most traditional sectors, companies were becoming more specialized and more competitive as they turned to exports.

Businesses were reaping the rewards of the free trade agreement signed with the United States in 1989, which became NAFTA in 1994. In the second half of the nineties, these businesses exported massively south of the border, making the most of strong American growth and a weak Canadian dollar. This golden age of Canadian exports did not last long, however, and came under threat from the rise of China in the following decade. China was able to put less-expensive products onto the market to compete with Canadian ones on the American market, while its demand for raw materials sent prices up—along with the Canadian dollar whose rise was also fuelled by skyrocketing oil prices. From the mid-2000s, Montreal industry therefore again came under pressure, but the damage would not be as widespread as in the seventies and eighties.

Montreal's economy was thus exposed to globalization, not only in international trade, but also in the world of investment. New waves of mergers and acquisitions swept away Quebec companies headquartered in Montreal, while others extended their networks abroad.

The revival of Montreal brought with it a new age of prosperity, and lower taxes increased disposable incomes. Early-retirement programs in the civil service and the broader public sector freed up jobs for young people, and, within a few years, unemployment had shrunk, both in the city and across the Montreal area.

The revival had a spectacular effect on the real estate market. In 1994, Montreal was still in shock following the collapse of property prices at the end of the 1990 recession. The market stagnated for a number of years, and the value of building permits in the Montreal area fell by half, reaching a nadir in 1995–1996. The housing vacancy rate climbed and owners looked for new ways to attract tenants. Things began to look up by decade's end, but the property market really took off in 2001. By 2006, building permits were worth three times as much as they had been ten years earlier and the market remained buoyant until 2012.

Close to the city centre, promoters snapped up every vacant lot and every parking lot to build condos. By the Lachine Canal or in Old Montreal, and in many other parts of the city, old warehouses and factories were converted into homes, while new blocks of luxury condos went up close to the downtown area. In no more than a few years, Montreal eliminated thousands of scars that blotched its urban landscape.

Gentrification—the process by which higher social classes move in to areas previously occupied by low-income groups—had already begun, but now moved up a gear. It was most visible in the Plateau and Mile End neighbourhoods, but also started to appear in the working-class neighbourhoods to the southwest, by the Lachine Canal.

A sizable chunk of new housing projects continued to be concentrated in the suburbs, although young couples now had to move further and further out of town to find affordable homes. The second ring of suburbs was where the action was at, in municipalities like Mirabel and Mascouche on the north shore or Saint-Basile-le-Grand on the south shore.

Contrasting populations

Between 1996 and 2001, the Montreal census metropolitan area (CMA) grew by only 100,000 inhabitants, but between 2001 and 2006, it increased by close to 210,000, reaching 3.6 million. Population growth was slightly less rapid during the next five years and the total stood at 3.8 million in 2011.

This increase was largely fuelled by immigration from abroad, since net migration with other parts of Canada was negative. Immigrants came mainly to live in the city itself, but since the city centre was continuing to lose residents to the surrounding area, the suburbs had the highest growth. The 450 area code was now shorthand for the suburbs around the island of Montreal. Experts noted growing differences in behaviour (politics, consumption, etc.) between people living there and those on the island of Montreal where the code was 514. Although the area had some small pockets where English and other languages were spoken, French was the number one language in the 450 dial code, an area that was home to half the people living in the CMA. With 368,000 inhabitants in 2006, Laval was the biggest suburban city and a case apart. On the south shore, Longueuil (229,000) trailed in its wake, while the rest of the CMA was made up of dozens of municipalities, big and small.

Due to migration from the city centre to the suburbs, the island of Montreal had fewer and fewer people who claimed French as their mother tongue, a fact that might have an impact on use of French in years to come. People who spoke languages other than French and English, and more generally, those whose ancestors did not hail from France or Great Britain and Ireland, remained concentrated on the island at the start of the twenty-first century, thus boosting its multicultural makeup. In 2001, 31 percent of people living on the island had a mother tongue other than French or English. In the suburbs, only Brossard (27.5 percent) and Laval (18 percent) are comparable from that standpoint.

At the turn of the twenty-first century, a new wave of immigration brought many Moroccans, Algerians, and Lebanese to Montreal. Many of them were Muslims, and mosques became a feature of the cityscape. Coming from countries that had been part of the former French empire or under French influence, these immigrants overwhelmingly chose to settle in Quebec and particularly Montreal when they moved to Canada, just like the thousands of men and women from France who have moved across the Atlantic. This gave Montreal quite a different makeup of immigrants compared to Canadian cities like Toronto and Vancouver. Moreover, immigrants from Asia (China, India, Pakistan, Sri Lanka, Korea, and elsewhere), although numerous, were proportionally fewer than in Canada's other two main metropolitan areas.

A closer look at geographical distribution reveals two phenomena. First, the biggest and oldest groups formed sorts of ethnic enclaves along Saint-Laurent boulevard, before migrating in waves to other parts of the city in the second half of the twentieth century. By the end of the century, Montrealers of Italian origin tended to live in Saint-Léonard and Rivière-des-Prairies, while the Jewish community has concentrated in Côte-Saint-Luc and nearby areas. Second, so many groups have arrived since the seventies that it is impossible for each to have its own neighbourhood. Instead, multicultural neighbourhoods have emerged, with groups of different backgrounds living side by side. Côte-des-Neiges, Parc-Extension, and certain parts of Saint-Laurent are prime examples.

These groups live in relative harmony, even when immigrants from countries historically in conflict with each other live side by side. Relations with the French-speaking majority also tend to be harmonious, with diversity now being recognized as part of Montreal's identity. Resistance has, however, appeared occasionally over the issue of reasonable accommodation for religious groups.

School-board reform has done much to improve inter-ethnic relations. School boards had been defined by religious denomination since the nineteenth century, with a Catholic school board on one side and a Protestant one on the other. The situation fell out of kilter with the city's religious diversity and the secular nature of public schools and hospitals, etc. Since the seventies, the need to divide school boards along linguistic rather than religious lines had been hotly debated. A constitutional amendment making this possible was passed in 1997, and the following year a French-language and an English-language school board were set up in Montreal. The suburbs followed suit.

Despite the return to a fair amount of prosperity, social divides have persisted in Montreal: in many areas of the city, a significant chunk of the population continues to live in poverty. Young men who dropped out of school have wound up in badly paid jobs, if not on unemployment and welfare; single-parent families, most often headed by mothers, are very often among the needy; and young people from visible minorities have found it harder than most to find employment. In short, Montreal has remained a city of contrasts, with social inequalities rife.

A time of political change

The 1994 Montreal elections marked a changing of the guard on the city council, with the defeat of the RCM and Jean Doré. The new mayor, Pierre Bourque, a former manager of Montreal's Botanical Garden, might have been a political novice, but he knew the city like the back of his hand. The Vision Montréal party he founded got the majority of seats, but the "maire jardinier" or "gardener mayor" faced hard times from the get-go, given the city's disastrous finances. His amateurish, hands-on approach soon had political observers wincing and led to defections from his party, but Pierre Bourque knew how to connect to Montrealers and remained very popular with voters, who swept him back to power in 1998.

Bourque revived Jean Drapeau's slogan of "Une île, une ville" (One Island, One City) and proposed the annexation of Montreal's neighbouring municipalities. Irony would have it that he would get his way, but would be unable to take advantage of the situation.

Montreal's relations with its suburbs was a hot topic throughout the nineties. One of the issues at stake was spreading the city's costs for downtown services and public facilities across the whole Montreal area.

At the start of the twenty-first century, two aspects of this issue were addressed. The first was managing the metropolitan area. The Communauté urbaine de Montréal (Montreal Urban Community), created in 1970, only took in part of the area and barely half the population living in and around Montreal. After much dithering, the Quebec government, led by Premier Lucien Bouchard, passed its solution to the problem in 2000. The CUM was abolished and replaced by the Communauté métropolitaine de Montréal. The CMM was put in charge of services and facilities for the metropolitan area, as well as regional planning and development.

The second aspect concerned municipal mergers. The Bouchard government was determined to reduce the number of municipalities in Quebec to get rid of duplication and improve administrative and fiscal efficiency.

Bill 170 provided for the creation of a new City of Montreal on January 1, 2002, which would encompass all the municipalities on the island. It also formed a single city on the south shore that would be known as Longueuil. In both cases, in 2001 a transition committee looked into reorganizing the services that these changes would entail. Elsewhere in the Montreal area, a number of municipalities followed suit and merged in twos and threes.

A number of towns on the island of Montreal resisted these forced mergers and tried, in vain, to have them overturned by the courts. Discontent also rumbled in a number of

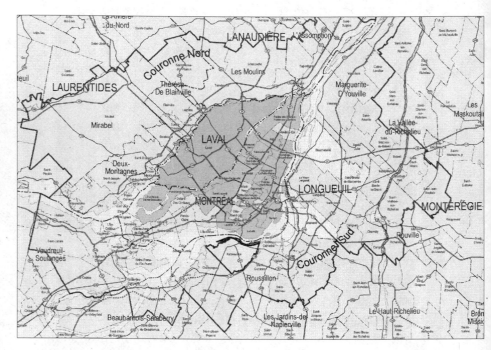

A REGIONAL BODY

This map shows the contours of the Communauté métropolitaine de Montréal, a regional body created in 2001 by the Quebec government. Its territory extends over 4360 square kilometres. The map also shows the two main suburban cities of Montreal: Laval and Longueuil.

(Communauté métropolitaine de Montréal)

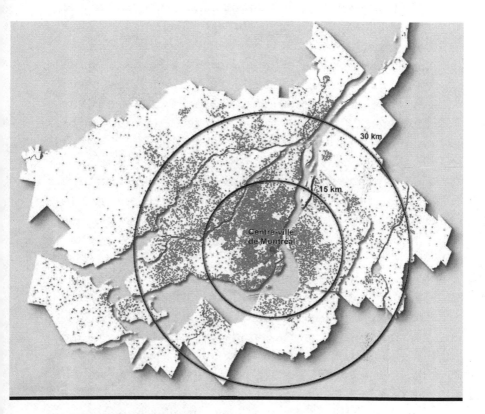

A SPRAWLING METROPOLIS

Early in the twenty-first century, the census metropolitan area of Montreal extends over a radius of more than 30 kilometres and houses almost four million people. It is the second largest in Canada, after Toronto, and about half the population of Quebec lives there.

municipalities on the south shore. The head of the Quebec Liberal Party, Jean Charest, promised to undo the mergers, if elected.

In November 2001, elections were held all the same to give the new city an administration. Mayor Bourque came away with a majority of seats in the former city, but lost out to Gérald Tremblay, head of the Union des citoyens et citoyennes de l'île de Montréal (Montreal Island Citizens' Union), who won more seats in the former suburbs and was elected mayor. It was something of a paradox that some members of the team now governing the new city were working towards its demise.

The law creating the new city included the creation of 27 boroughs (*arrondissements*). Managed by elected officials, these boroughs provide community services and keep the municipal administration in touch with the people. In other words, the boroughs were created to devolve powers away from the centre. Boroughs had to manage local budgets, services, and staff. The Tremblay administration took this devolution process a step further, with the officials elected to manage boroughs later becoming borough mayors.

In 2003, Jean Charest became Quebec premier and kept his word on allowing demergers. The tightly overseen procedure called for referendums to be held, the results of which would be valid only if participation rates were at least 35 percent. In June 2004, 15 former municipalities on the island—all but one of which were on the West Island—were given the go-ahead to demerge from Montreal. On the south shore, four former towns chose to separate from Longueuil. These reconstituted towns did not enjoy as broad a range of powers as before, however. On the island, they were in a minority against Montreal in the new agglomeration council that managed budgets and common services.

When the dust settled, Montreal kept a number of its former suburban towns, including Saint-Laurent, Outremont, Verdun, LaSalle, Montréal-Nord, Anjou, and Saint-Léonard. It brought almost 90 percent of the people living on the island under its umbrella.

In November 2005, an election was held that would test the new city's mettle. Gérald Tremblay was re-elected mayor and his councillors won a majority of seats—in the boroughs of the old city, as well. It was a disaster for Pierre Bourque, who left municipal politics soon afterwards, and a result that proved Montreal had begun to integrate old and new. Mayor Tremblay won again in 2009, but with a reduced majority.

In just a few years, Montreal had undergone a series of sweeping political changes, and its leaders had to adapt quickly to this new reality. Montreal's expansion had given it new stature, and the means to become the metropolitan leader.

In the fall of 2012, the city's pride was dealt a severe blow. A provincial inquiry commission on corruption in the construction industry revealed an extended graft system in Montreal's public works. A crisis ensued with the resignation of Mayor Tremblay and the partial collapse of his party. A new chapter in the lively political history of Montreal was opening up.

A SOCIAL HOTSPOT

A student protest against a tuition-fee hike attracted a huge crowd for a march on Sherbrooke street, on March 22, 2012. Since at least the nineteenth century, public demonstrations have been a feature of urban life in Montreal. The city has always been a kind of social laboratory where new ideas and protests are expressed vocally.

(Photo: Jacques Nadeau)

Conclusion

This look at Montreal's history has set out various milestones along the way. On a piece of land that once belonged to the Iroquoians, a tiny missionary colony took root in 1642. After difficult beginnings, it became a bustling trading centre, built first around the fur trade, then around a diversified commercial system. From the mid-nineteenth century onwards, industrialization transformed the small town into a sprawling city abuzz with activity. Then, over the course of the twentieth century, the development of the services sector broadened the city's role. The Swinging Sixties came and went, and Montreal went through a period of major upheavals that sparked serious efforts at modernization.

From its beginnings, Montreal enjoyed a host of advantages, not least its location on the St. Lawrence River. But in order for these advantages to be driven home, Montreal required a great deal of entrepreneurship and no small amount of creative thinking from a host of men and women who were devoted to their city and determined to equip it with the most vibrant of institutions. Paul de Chomedey de Maisonneuve and Jeanne Mance led by example, but each generation that followed supplied its own contingent of visionaries. Behind the big names, millions of ordinary men and women, business people, members of the Church, artisans, factory workers, office workers, intellectuals, and artists worked in their own special way—often in obscurity—to make Montreal the exceptional city it is today.

Throughout its long history, one of the key features behind Montreal's *je ne sais quoi* has been its French roots. The French of New France became *Les Canadiens*, then French Canadians, and finally Quebecers over the years, but whatever they have been called, they have always played a crucial role in every stage of the city's development. They have marked every facet of life in Montreal. They developed an original culture, constantly looking to bridge their French heritage and Quebec culture and the cultures of the many people from all over the world who have come to call Montreal home. They made their city the beating heart of modern Quebec.

For two and a half centuries, the city has also absorbed British and English-Canadian influences, and that interaction with French-speaking Montreal has created a society like no other. The sizable British contingent made a lasting contribution to the city, shaping its economy, institutions, and architecture. Then, the past century saw Jews and Italians—and later groups from all kinds of cultural backgrounds—make contributions of their own.

Another striking feature of Montreal's history is its Americanness. Though European in origin, the city quickly adapted to the realities of life in North America. From the days of New France, Montrealers demonstrated a continental vision that they have kept ever since. They borrowed and benefited from the culture and technology of those around them—first the Aboriginal peoples, then their American neighbours to the south.

Montreal has therefore been—and continues to be—a welcoming city, a melting pot where diverse cultures feel right at home, a place where people from distant lands and diverse ethnic and social backgrounds settle down and live together. It is a city of dialogue and exchange, where people, ideas, goods, money, and technology circulate freely. Of course, many other cities in North America boast similar features, but something special sets Montreal apart, no doubt due to the French and English worlds it is home to. That's what makes it such a fascinating city.

Selected Readings

Bibliography

Burgess, Joanne, Louise Dechêne, Paul-André Linteau and Jean-Claude Robert. *Clés pour l'histoire de Montréal. Bibliographie.* Montreal: 1992.

Surveys

Atherton, William H. *Montreal, 1535-1914.* Montreal: 1914. 3 vol.

Benoît, Michèle and Roger Gratton. *Pignon sur rue. Les quartiers de Montréal.* Montreal: 1991.

Blanchard, Raoul. *Montréal, esquisse de géographie urbaine.* Montreal: 1992.

Cooper, John Irwin. *Montreal: A Brief History.* Montreal: 1969.

Dechêne, Louise. *Habitants and Merchants in Seventeenth-Century Montreal.* Montreal: 1992.

Dechêne, Louise. « La croissance de Montréal au xviiie siècle », *Revue d'histoire de l'Amérique française*, 27, 2 (September 1973), p. 163-179.

Fougères, Dany, ed. *Histoire de Montréal et de sa région.* Quebec: 2012. 2 vol.

Higgins, Benjamin. *The Rise and Fall? of Montreal. A Case Study of Urban Growth, Regional Economic Expansion and National Development.* Moncton: 1986.

Lachance, André. *La vie urbaine en Nouvelle-France.* Montreal: 1987.

Landry, Yves, ed. *Pour le Christ et le roi. La vie au temps des premiers Montréalais.* Montreal: 1992.

LINTEAU, Paul-André. *Histoire de Montréal depuis la Confédération.* Montreal: 2000.

LINTEAU, Paul-André and Jean-Claude ROBERT. *Le Montréal préindustriel (1760-1850)/Pre-industrial Montreal (1760-1850).* Ottawa: 1980.

MARSAN, Jean-Claude. *Montreal in Evolution: Historical Analysis of the Development of Montreal's Architecture and Urban Environment.* Montreal: 1981.

ROBERT, Jean-Claude. *Montréal (1821-1871). Aspects de l'urbanisation.* Doctoral dissertation, Université de Paris I, 1977.

ROBERT, Jean-Claude. *Atlas historique de Montréal.* Montreal: 1994.

RUMILLY, Robert. *Histoire de Montréal.* Montreal: 1970-1974. 5 vol.

Monographs

BRADBURY, Bettina. *Working Families: Age, Gender, and Daily Survival in Industrializing Montreal.* Toronto: 1993.

BRADBURY, Bettina and Tamara MYERS, ed. *Negotiating Identities in 19th- and 20th-Century Montreal.* Vancouver: 2005.

BRADBURY, Bettina. *Wife to Widow: Lives, Laws, and Politics in Nineteenth-Century Montreal.* Vancouver: 2011.

DAGENAIS, Michèle. *Des pouvoirs et des hommes. L'administration municipale de Montréal, 1900-1950.* Montreal: 2000.

DESLANDRES, Dominique, John A. DICKINSON and Ollivier HUBERT, ed. *Les Sulpiciens de Montréal. Une histoire de pouvoir et de discrétion, 1657-2007.* Montreal: 2007.

DROUILLY, Pierre. *L'espace social de Montréal, 1951-1991.* Sillery: 1996.

DROUIN, Martin. *Le combat du patrimoine à Montréal (1973-2003).* Quebec: 2005.

DURFLINGER, Serge Marc. *Fighting from Home: The Second World War in Verdun, Quebec.* Vancouver: 2006.

FAHRNI, Magda. *Household Politics: Montreal Families and Postwar Reconstruction.* Toronto: 2005.

FYSON, Donald. *Magistrates, Police, and People: Everyday Criminal Justice in Quebec and Lower Canada, 1764-1837.* Toronto: 2006.

FOUGÈRES, Dany. *L'approvisionnement en eau à Montréal. Du privé au public, 1796-1865.* Quebec: 2004.

GOURNAY, Isabelle and France VANLAETHEM, ed. *Montreal Metropolis, 1880-1930.* Toronto: 1998.

LAMBERT, Phyllis and Alan STEWART, ed. *Opening the Gates of Eighteenth-Century Montreal.* Montreal: 1992.

LAUZON, Gilles and Madeleine FORGET, ed. *Old Montreal: History Through Heritage.* Quebec: 2004.

LEVINE, Marc V. *The Reconquest of Montreal: Language Policy and Social Change in a Bilingual City.* Philadelphia: 1990.

LEWIS, Robert. *Manufacturing Montreal: The Making of an Industrial Landscape, 1850 to 1930.* Baltimore: 2000.

LINTEAU, Paul-André. *Sainte-Catherine Street: At the Heart of Montreal Life.* Montreal,: 2010.

LORTIE, André, ed. *The 60s: Montreal Thinks Big.* Montreal: 2004.

McNICOLL, Claire. *Montréal. Une société multiculturelle.* Paris: 1993.

PENDERGAST, James F. and Bruce G. TRIGGER, ed. *Cartier's Hochelaga and the Dawson Site.* Montreal: 1972.

OLSON, Sherry and Patricia THORNTON. *Peopling the North American City: Montreal 1840-1900.* Montreal: 2011.

POITRAS, Claire. *La cité au bout du fil. Le téléphone à Montréal de 1879 à 1930.* Montreal: 2000.

SANCTON, Andrew. *Governing the Island of Montreal: Language Differences and Metropolitan Politics.* Berkeley: 1985.

TRUDEL, Marcel. *Montréal: la formation d'une société, 1642-1663.* Montreal: 1976.

TULCHINSKY, Gerald. *The River Barons. Montreal Businessmen and the Growth of Industry and Transportation, 1837-1853.* Toronto: 1977.

VANLAETHEM, France, Sarah MARCHAND, Paul-André LINTEAU and Jacques-André CHARTRAND. *Place Ville Marie: Montreal's Shining Landmark.* Montreal: 2012.

YOUNG, Brian J. *In Its Corporate Capacity: the Seminary of Montreal as a Business Institution, 1816-1876.* Montreal: 1986.

Index

Printed by Imprimerie Gauvin
Gatineau, Québec